CUMBERLAND COUNTY

COUNTY

❯ · N E W J E R S E Y · ❮

CUMBERLAND COUNTY

COUNTY

※ NEW JERSEY ※

265 YEARS *of* HISTORY

CHARLES HARRISON

Charleston   London

THE
History
PRESS

Published by The History Press
Charleston, SC 29403
www.historypress.net

Copyright © 2013 by Charles H. Harrison
All rights reserved

First published 2013

Manufactured in the United States

ISBN 978.1.60949.776.7

Library of Congress CIP data applied for.

CONTENTS

CONTENTS

HAPPY BIRTHDAY!

The year 1748 became the official birth year for the sovereign of Great Britain, who that year happened to be George II. What better way for the colonial legislature to say happy birthday to George than to break off a sizeable chunk of Salem County and name it in honor of his younger son, William, the Duke of Cumberland. No matter, of course, that William was better known in some places and by some people as "Butcher Cumberland." He earned the title as commander of British forces in 1746 that defeated—some historians say massacred—Scottish highlanders commanded by Bonnie Prince Charlie at the Battle of Culloden.

Of course, if the ordinary settlers of the newly named county were pleased at the time about the separation from Salem and sort of okay about the connection to the "butcher," they became very unhappy about a quarter century later with everyone and everything associated with the British Crown. Quite a number of those British subjects in the relatively new county—and not a few of them rather important and well known— decorated themselves as Lenape Indians and defiantly burned a cellar full of British tea.

Cumberland County Patriots truly distinguished themselves (and without the war paint) when they returned to Salem County on a bad day in March 1778 and helped save the day for the Salem militiamen trying to hold on to the bridge at Quinton against a superior British force.

At the Revolution's end, the families of Cumberland County—a number of them having transplanted themselves from New England and a few who had come from as far away as Sweden—got down to the hard work of making their home county one of the prize counties of the new state of New Jersey. They plowed the land and planted acres upon acres of vegetables, wheat, shrubs and flowers. They fished in two great rivers and then discovered oysters in the Delaware Bay, soon making a world-renowned industry out of the harvesting and processing of those oysters.

Over the years, the residents of Cumberland County organized themselves into fourteen communities, and those communities grew and prospered. Families whose ancestors had migrated from New England or emigrated from Sweden were joined by new families from places with Spanish names.

Sometime in this year of 2013—265 years after the county's breakaway from Salem—the 153,000 residents of Cumberland County need to pause in their daily routines and remember with gratitude all those men and women who have made this anniversary so worth celebrating.

Chapter 1

ALWAYS THE RIVERS

S ure, four-lane highways and airport runways now connect Cumberland County with the world far beyond its borders, but those connections are fairly recent when time is measured in millennia. On the other hand, the Cohansey and Maurice Rivers have been moving people in and out of Cumberland County since, well, since there were rivers and people.

Today, the two rivers, both of which originate in Salem County and flow south into the Delaware River, roughly divide Cumberland County into three sections. The land west of the Cohansey River consists mostly of farmland. The center section between the rivers boasts the cities of Bridgeton and Millville, and the section east of the Maurice River consists primarily of Vineland and the Peaslee Wildlife Management Area.

Long ago—eons before helicopters flew into Millville Airport and centuries before tea burned in Greenwich—Unalachtigo families of the Lenape people of the Delaware tribe lived, worked, played and died along the banks of the rivers (*kithanes*).

The land was mostly forested except for where the Lenape families gathered in small villages along the rivers, which served as their ready source of water for cooking and bathing and perhaps was where children played on the banks. Also, the Lenape men tied their dugout canoes to trees close to the river. Unlike western Indians, who lived in teepees, Lenape families lived in huts made of tree saplings that were first planted straight into the ground and then bent at the top to form a roof frame that was then covered in sheets of tree bark.

East Point Lighthouse. *Courtesy of Lummis Research Library.*

Game was everywhere, and the rivers were filled with fish. Lenape men caught the fish with the aid of nets, bows and arrows or weirs. The weir was a V-shaped dam made of stones, with the point of the "V" angled downstream. The Lenape men would go upstream and then drag downstream a net made from tree branches or Indian hemp. Fish would be pushed or pulled downstream to the "dam," where they could be speared or clubbed.

In the summer, Lenape families, like many Cumberland clans in modern times, would gather together whatever they needed for spending long, warm days and nights at the shore. They set up camps along the bay and feasted on oysters, clams, crabs and mussels. They also were smart enough to dry or smoke enough clams, crabs and mussels that they could pack them up at the end of summer and feast on them during the cold months ahead.

Lenape families, particularly the men, spent a lot of time in their dugout canoes on the rivers. The typical canoe was twelve feet long, but some were as long as forty feet. The canoe started as a fallen tree that was hollowed out first by heaping on burning coals and then by scraping away the charred wood. The process took a long time and much effort, and one might assume that the Lenape man of centuries past kept his canoe tied to the riverbank longer than the typical male of the twenty-first century keeps his automobile in the garage.

Lenape families were pretty self-sufficient. They built and furnished the homes where they raised their children. The men hunted game in the plentiful woods and caught fish in the rivers; their mates tended gardens and harvested corn, beans and squash, as well as some pretty bad tobacco.

Then came the white man and woman and their children. In the beginning, they were self-sufficient, too. The men hunted in the woods and fished in the rivers they called Cohansey (after a Lenape chief) and the Maurice (after a prince of the House of Orange). The white women tended vegetable gardens that looked a lot like those tended by Lenape women.

Of course, while the first white settlers learned about living on the land and the rivers from Lenape families (and sometimes *bought* their land for a handful of trinkets), they also wanted to replicate as best they could some aspects of the life and times they left behind in Europe. This meant that the houses they built along the banks of the thirty-mile-long Cohansey River and the thirty-nine-mile Maurice River resembled the houses they grew up in and were almost not at all like huts made of tree saplings.

These first and later settlers along the rivers wanted and needed farmland to provide life's essentials for their families, as well as, perhaps, enough to share with friends and sell to others who needed and paid for what they grew and raised on their land. Over time, of course, the new Americans found better ways to take the water out of the Cohansey and Maurice Rivers, and they also discovered new uses for the free-flowing and reliable streams: power for industry.

When the Lenape Indians lived along the two rivers, they didn't worry very much about whether the rivers might somehow be affected by their simple way of life, and they didn't lose any sleep trying to predict what Mother Nature might have in store for the rivers and them from year to year or decade to decade.

By the eighteenth and nineteenth centuries, however, families living along the rivers had become concerned about how they might secure their land and protect it from slipping—foot by foot and yard by yard—into the rivers. In his 1869 history of Cumberland County, Lucius Q.C. Elmer wrote that as early as 1760, laws were being passed that required property owners along the Cohansey River, through their "joint efforts," to erect banks that would define the river and protect landowners' property. He continued: "Until within the last thirty years [going back to 1839]…the reclaimed meadows, notwithstanding the great expense generally attending the maintenance of the banks, were almost indispensable and commanded a high price. Those on Maurice River, which are easily renovated by the muddy sediment deposited from the water when allowed to flow over them, are of an excellent quality and are still of much value."

Among others who addressed concerns about land erosion and land reclamation was Salem County native Robert Gibbons Johnson. Writing in the *American Farmer* in 1826, Johnson suggested that the best way to protect valuable farmland from becoming mud at the bottom of the rivers was to build and maintain dikes and banks. Of course, he and others who also made the same case knew that building and maintaining a diking or banking system took time, money and intelligence. Farmers and other landowners who ventured into reclamation, Johnson argued, had to be familiar with simple engineering methods, as well as cycles of nature, if they were to have a successful outcome. For example, they had to know how deep to dig ditches and how high to build riverbanks.

The theory proclaimed by early and later authorities about maintaining the banks of the rivers and the farmland, homesteads and industries that they protected noted that the height and strength of the banks needed to be proportional to the depth and weight of the water they were designed to hold back or keep in check. Also important, they said, was to make sure that the embankments were smooth enough that they presented the least possible resistance to river currents.

Since the nineteenth century, of course, an increasing population and even more industry have often interacted with the Cohansey and Maurice Rivers in ways that have adversely affected both the people and the rivers. In many locations, for example, dikes or embankments that dated from the nineteenth and twentieth centuries—or even earlier—have been allowed to fall into disrepair.

Sometimes, it seems, governments have made it more difficult and costlier to maintain the integrity of the rivers and their embankments. For example, in 1972, the Burcham family wanted to repair the Maurice River bank on their property near Millville that had been damaged by a hurricane. They thought that they would use mud dredged from the river bottom as they and generations before them had done to reinforce or replace riverbanks. The State of New Jersey advised them that they could no longer use mud from the river bottom. Consequently, they had to use a combination of concrete, oyster and clamshells, a costlier solution.

Fast-forward to the summer of 2012. Edward Sheppard, whose ancestor dressed up like a Lenape Indian and burned British tea on the Greenwich square, was quoted by the South Jersey Media Group's Sunday newspaper as complaining that "in another 30 years, there won't be a Greenwich,"

Sheppard's Landing as it looked centuries ago. *Courtesy of Lummis Research Library.*

because it is being steadily washed away by the Cohansey River. According to the newspaper account, "Greenwich is regularly flooded by salt water from the bay because of faulty dikes, which have historically protected the town from the Cohansey River. Now, the river that helped to establish Greenwich as an early New Jersey port is looking to claim the township."

Since at least the beginning of this century, reported the newspaper, dike maintenance has been an issue in Greenwich and elsewhere along the Cohansey River. Insofar as the town's residents are concerned, the newspaper reported, "the dike issue has had Greenwich on its knees. High tides, storms and full moons mean damaged property and inconvenience for its 804 residents. Despite promises from elected officials, nothing has yet been done to stop the flooding." Sheppard has not given up trying to get local, state or federal authorities to solve the problem. "This dike issue I'm not going to give up on," he is quoted as saying. "It's either going to get fixed or I'm going to die trying." He's in his late sixties.

If, as the newspaper and Mr. Sheppard point out, the Cohansey River is now gobbling up precious land, studies by agencies of Rutgers University and other federal and state bodies predict a more dismal future. Noted one report: "Perhaps the greatest threat to the Cohansey and indeed to New Jersey's entire coastal region is the vulnerability of its coastal habitats to sea level rise and severe coastal storms. Sea level rise is a well documented reality that is already impacting New Jersey's coastline and the Cohansey River."

All the news is not bad. In the mid-1980s, state, county and local authorities were fearful that controversial development proposals might threaten the Maurice River. As a result of their concern and subsequent action, the Maurice River has been designated by federal and state governments as a scenic river worth careful attention and saving.

If Lenape families were to return this year to ply the Cohansey and Maurice Rivers in their dugout canoes, they could not and would not wish to adapt to the life they would find along the riverbanks in the twenty-first century. However, they might appreciate that modern society tries very hard to keep the waters of the rivers clean, and they would notice that men, women and children still go out on boats to sit most of the day dangling their fishing lines into the running water.

It's almost certain, particularly if they were boating on the Maurice River, that they might look to the sky and marvel at a very familiar sight: the magnificent bald eagle.

Chapter 2

THANK YOU, LENAPE INDIANS

T he first settlers found an unbroken forest covering the land in all of this portion of the state, except the Indian clearings, which were few and of no large extent."

That's how Thomas Cushing and Charles Sheppard begin the section about agriculture in Cumberland County in their 1883 book, *History of the Counties of Gloucester, Salem and Cumberland New Jersey*. "[E]xcept the Indian clearings" is the key part of that sentence because it was the Lenape Indians who first occupied what became Cumberland County, and it was those Indians who taught white settlers how to clear land and raise crops. Many, if not most, of the early settlers from Europe came either from cities or villages, where they tended small gardens consisting mostly of flowers. They went to market to buy whatever vegetables they served their families, and they went somewhere else to purchase meat, fish, hay, straw and so on.

What Cumberland's white settlers learned from the Lenape men was how to clear land by girdling trees—that is, cutting off a wide strip of bark, which would eventually result in the trees dying. Some larger trees were burned. The settlers learned from Lenape women how to plant corn and beans in rows and fertilize the soil with wood ashes, as well as parts of fish and game not normally eaten by humans.

The next key paragraph in Cushing and Sheppard's book begins by pointing out that "the means used for tilling the soil were crude and inefficient." Remember, most of these settlers had never tilled soil except to dig smallish holes for smallish flowers and plants. "The [settlers'] plow was made of wood throughout, the team was generally oxen, and plowing the ground was scarcely more than scratching the surface." The following sentence reveals much about early, primitive agriculture as practiced by the first white settlers: "Little manure was made, no fertilizers were used, lime for agricultural purposes was not thought of, and marl was not discovered."

Cushing and Sheppard explained what often happened to the farmland tilled by early settlers and first-time farmers: "For the want of manure and fertilizers and a better system of farming, a great deal of the land became poorer day by day. The portion tilled was cropped until it was exhausted, when it was abandoned, and new ground cleared, only to go through the same agricultural methods." The authors described what usually resulted after the settlers exhausted their farmland: "Between 1815 and 1830 many of the inhabitants sold their worn-out lands and moved to Ohio, Indiana, and Illinois, whose virgin soils, much of them without any trees to be cut, offered many inducements to those who saw their lands in [Cumberland County] becoming poorer with each succeeding year."

Actions that saved farmland and agriculture in the county, according to the authors, included "the raising of upland hay, especially clover, the rotation of crops, the application of lime to the soil, and the discovery and use of marl." Marl is a claylike, finely textured soil found chiefly in a wide strip that extends from around Perth Amboy in northeast New Jersey to Salem and Cumberland Counties in the southwest.

Agriculture and good farming practices were first widely promoted in the county by the Cumberland County Agricultural and Horticultural Society in 1823. The first fair—referred to as an exhibition—was held on November 18, 1823. According to Cushing and Sheppard, "A light fall of snow the night before interfered somewhat with its success, but the display of cattle and hogs was good, and a large number of people attended." The second exhibition was better, and the third in 1825 ran for two days and was even more successful. The society's report about the third exhibition noted that "[t]he display of stock was far superior to that of any former exhibition; and from the vast collection of farmers and citizens from different parts of the county, and from the neighboring counties who attended to witness the scene, the society felt highly gratified." Today, the annual fair is held in July.

Also today, as is the case with almost everything, much about agriculture—what is grown and harvested and how it is processed and marketed—has changed. Of course, the market largely determines what is grown. Wesley Kline, county agricultural agent for commercial vegetable

Wesley Kline, Cumberland County agricultural agent for commercial vegetable production. *Photo by Stephan A. Harrison.*

production in 2012, explained how the market has changed and how that change has affected what Cumberland County farmers grow and harvest.

One of the major changes, said Mr. Kline, took place when Seabrook Farms—once called the "greatest vegetable factory on earth"—was sold or divided up. A number of the farmers who depended on Seabrook to buy their farm products switched from growing vegetables to growing nursery stock and/or sod. Mr. Kline also pointed out that the major food processors in the county and South Jersey, such as Campbell's, Ritters and Heinz, for example, moved west. The companies' reasons for moving out west included the benefit of a warmer, year-round climate, particularly in California; much higher yields; cheaper land prices; and less regulation.

Today, according to Mr. Kline, many or most of the major farms in the county grow corn, wheat, soybeans and hay as rotational crops, meaning that most of those farms also grow some vegetables. "Cumberland County is sort of divided in half, east and west of State Highway 55. West of 55 [the major portion of the county] you have both field crop and vegetable growers. East of Route 55, you're really talking about mostly vegetable growers." The reasons are probably twofold, he said. "Part of the reason is tradition. In the eastern part of the state and going into Atlantic County you have primarily the small, Italian-American growers. That's where Italian farmers originally settled, so that's part of it. The acreage per farm is lower in the eastern part of the county, and, I think, that also has to do with tradition."

Cumberland County farmers began shipping vegetables by rail into Philadelphia sometime in the early 1900s, Mr. Kline said. Then, of course, Campbell Soup Company in Camden, Ritters in Bridgeton and other canneries came along later and bought vegetables from Cumberland County farmers. "We're still a major exporter of vegetables," he said. Lettuce, peppers, tomatoes, parsley, basil and dill are some of the major crops exported out of Cumberland County. In the early spring, he added, Cumberland County vegetables may be shipped north to Ontario, Canada. In the summer months, local farmers may ship their products mostly south because the growing season is essentially over in that part of the country.

The Vineland Auction, which is the largest of its kind on the East Coast, has been the place where Cumberland County farmers have marketed their produce over the years. In the past, the annual sales out of the Vineland Auction have been as high as $20 million a year, said Mr. Kline. The auction now has fewer members than it once did simply because of farm consolidation. Also, he said, more farmers today ship direct to wholesalers or supermarket chains rather than go through the auction. One of the advantages of farmers selling direct to wholesalers or supermarkets, said Mr. Kline, is that they know exactly what they're going to get per acre or per ton.

As far as trends in local agriculture go, Mr. Kline said that one is the diversity in the kinds of crops grown, particularly vegetables. A major change is the use of drip irrigation, especially for vegetables. It is a more efficient use of water, and drip irrigation also produces a better quality in crops. In the past, he said, when water from overhead sprinklers or rain splashed onto crops, sand or dirt also was often splashed on. When that happened, farmers often got a lower price for their products.

"I think we'll be seeing more protective agriculture," said Mr. Kline, "for instance, the use of high plastic tunnels. What this means is putting a rain shelter over the crop. It's kind of like a greenhouse but without the heat. Farmers get a longer season by starting earlier in the spring and going longer in the fall."

What is the future for agriculture in Cumberland County? Mr. Kline pointed out that a considerable number of acres in the eastern part of the county that are now being farmed are actually under contract to developers who will likely build houses on that farmland if and when the economy improves.

Chapter 3

NEW SWEDEN IS AN OLDE MEMORY

In the middle of the seventeenth century, when Cumberland was still part of Salem and settlers from Sweden, the Netherlands and England settled land that they took from the Lenape Indians, the entire Swedish colony on either side of the Delaware River numbered fewer than 500 persons. Incidentally, some (perhaps many) of those listed as being Swedes were actually Finns. Johan Printz, the rotund governor of New Sweden in the mid-1600s, reported back to Sweden that the shortage of settlers from the "old country" was an ongoing problem. He noted in 1644 that New Sweden was inhabited by only 105 males. One-fourth of that number was soldiers, most of them assigned to Fort Elfsborg on the east bank of the Delaware River.

The numbers hadn't increased all that much a century later. According to the authors of the book *The Rise and Fall of New Sweden*, in the last half of the eighteenth century, in all of the land on both sides of the Delaware River that was called New Sweden, those persons who were "acquainted with the Swedish language" numbered only 1,195. Of that number, only 31 lived in what is today Cumberland County. These Swedes lived primarily along the Maurice River, also known as the Assveticons.

What and why and where was New Sweden? As was the case for nearly all the "News" in America (e.g., New England and New Jersey), New Sweden came into being when adventuresome individuals and families—and, more importantly, men with business and/or governmental connections—went in search of adventure, new beginnings, new sources of nearly everything wanted or needed in Europe and, of course, new sources of income.

A rebuilt Swedish storage building in Greenwich. *Courtesy of Lummis Research Library.*

In the case of New Sweden, for example, New Jersey historian Peter O. Wacker pointed out that in the beginning, the area that became New Sweden was explored initially to determine whether the Swedes and the Dutch could do business with the Lenape Indians:

> *In 1638, Swedish and Dutch merchants, who had formed the New Sweden Company under the aegis of the Swedish Crown, mounted an expedition to the area and established Fort Christiana* [near present Wilmington, Delaware]. *As with the Dutch, primary interest lay in the development of commerce with the Indians and in settling the west bank of the* [Delaware] *river. It was not until 1641 that the company added land, purchased from the Lenape, on the east bank of the river.*

The territory abutting the river that became New Sweden included the land on the west side from Cape Henlopen to a point opposite Trenton and on the east side from Cape May to the Raccoon Creek in Gloucester County.

The following year, 1642, Johan Printz was appointed governor of New Sweden. According to the book *New Jersey as a Colony and as a State: One of the Original Thirteen*, Printz had the following instructions from the guardians of Swedish Queen Christina: "[He] was directed to preserve the fur trade monopoly, to stimulate the cultivation of tobacco, foster grazing, arborculture, viniculture, silk, salt production and fishing. To his care was left the maintenance of the Swedish Lutheran religion, the education of the youth, and the Christianization of the Indians."

The population in all of New Sweden in 1645 was about two hundred men, women and children. "Because the population was so small, [New Sweden] was sparsely settled," according to the book *The Rise and Fall of New Sweden*. "The new settlements were scattered, principally along the waterways [such as the Maurice River and its tributaries] in the recently conquered wilderness. People did not live in villages as they did in Sweden [and as the Lenape did]; the farms were located alone and surrounded by their holdings. The houses were constructed of logs, and the cracks were filled with clay."

As previously noted, regardless of their small numbers in Cumberland County at any one time, many (perhaps most) of the Swedish families who originally settled here chose to live along the banks of the Maurice River, principally in the area now known as Port Elizabeth. Gabriel Thomas, a Friend (Quaker) from England who spent some time in the area, reported later that the Maurice River banks were "where the Swedes used to kill the geese in great numbers for their feathers only, leaving their carcasses behind them."

Reverend Nicholas Collin, when he came down the Maurice River from the much larger Swedish settlement on the Raccoon Creek in Gloucester County in about 1730, said later that he "rode astray in the wilderness all afternoon" in search of the Swedish colonists, who in turn were in search of and need of a pastor.

For some time, the Swedish settlers on the Maurice River depended on the pastors of churches at Swedesboro and Penns Neck to come down the Maurice River occasionally to preach the word and perform rituals. More often than not, Cumberland County settlers had to travel to one of those two churches in Gloucester County if they wanted to worship with the larger body of their countrymen. It wasn't until 1743 that the Swedish settlement in Cumberland County became a separate parish, and it wasn't until two years later that a church was built where services were conducted, making it so area residents no longer had to travel to Swedesboro.

Even though the Cumberland County settlement had its own church by 1745, the congregation still was dependent on the pastor of one of the Gloucester County churches. According to the book *The Swedes and Finns in New Jersey*:

Because [the church in Port Elizabeth] *was one of the pastorless churches in Swedish–New Jersey history, the church, when it was finally completed, was served by the Moravian brethren, peripatetic missionaries among both the Swedes and the Germans. Paul Bryzelius, a Moravian who had been holding services at Raccoon and Penns Neck, preached the first sermon in the new church in 1745. Another Moravian, the Swedish Count Abraham Reinicke, performed the dedicatory service the following year. Swedish* [language] *was still used by the preachers in 1748.*

By the middle of the eighteenth century, Count Reinicke and others visiting the Swedish settlements in Cumberland County and elsewhere in the area that had been New Sweden complained that "the English are evidently swallowing up the [Swedish settlers.] The Swedish language is so corrupted that, if I did not know the English [language,] it would be impossible to understand the language of my dear Sweden." According to one account, only one-third of the Swedish settlers could still understand the Swedish language by the middle of the eighteenth century.

The Swedish families who settled in Cumberland County may sometimes have been without a pastor in their church or may have begun speaking more in English than Swedish, but they made the most of the land they had settled. According to the New Jersey Historical Society, the settlers planted and harvested various grains and vegetables and raised cattle and hogs. Swedes and Finns made the most of the forest of conifer. They used the wood from these trees to build their houses, barns and other buildings. They also built boats to carry boards, charcoal and other products to Philadelphia, and "some experts believe that the Delaware River's famous cargo-carrying Durham boats and the keelboats on western rivers were developed by Swedes."

By the eighteenth century, New Sweden, as a separate entity, no longer existed, but the influence and contributions of the Swedish and Finnish settlers have carried on even into the twenty-first century.

Chapter 4

"THE LORD OF HOSTS IS ON OUR SIDE"

I t was May 19, 1776, a Sunday morning, and the Deerfield Presbyterian Church, newly built of sandstone to replace the original log edifice, was probably crowded. Reverend Enoch Green stood in front of the congregation. Some people may have thought that the Reverend Mr. Green looked particularly wan, as if he had not slept well the night before. He looked out at the congregants; a number of the men were in the uniform of the county militia.

"At a day of publick danger and calamity," he began, "the duty of every man is to contribute to the common defence and safety. Such a day is present, when our dearest rights are muted." Then he announced that the "officers of the Battalion have been pleased to elect me to the office of Chaplain."

Reverend Mr. Green looked out at his congregation. "We have now arrived at the alarming crisis, when we must either bravely contend or basely submit. America, I fear, has seen her best days; her golden age is spent, for, until this threatening period, happy was America when protected and beloved by Britain; happy was Britain in the affection, veneration and commerce of America. But now, alas, the endearing ties have burst asunder. Britain stains her hands in the blood of her faithful brethren and sons."

He continued: "We desire not, we seek not independence; we wish to be allied with our parent state, never to be divorced. We are ready to serve the King, labour for him, pray for him, fight for him and die for him, but never be enslaved by him. Englishmen must be free men. It would be much more consistent in the character of a preacher of the Gospel of peace, as well as

The Dunn-Stratton House in Millville dates from 1778. *Photo by Stephan A. Harrison.*

my natural temper, to exhort for peace." However, he accused the British ministry of "a lust for power, glory, wealth and revenge," and then, perhaps reluctantly, he called on his fellow Americans to "oppose force with force, or we shall never redeem the British Ministry to reason."

Reverend Green spoke for a good long time. He was about to conclude his remarks when he recalled English history and noted that "the Whigs have always gained the day, and as long as the House of Hanover was true to the interests of the Whigs, glory and prosperity followed them, but now King George has turned Tory; he has abandoned the cause of his best friends and has become the cruel murderer of his faithful subjects and is employing all his force and policy to destroy that body of men that raised his family to the throne." With obvious reference to the factions then competing, he said that he hoped that local Tories would be "brought over by force or persuasion. A Tory must be either knave or fool!" Reverend Green then ended his sermon.

In November of that year, 1776, two companies of Cumberland County militia were formed under the command of Colonel David Potter of Bridgeton. In September of the next year, the British captured and occupied Philadelphia. According to the historians Thomas Cushing and Charles Sheppard, at about that time, Brigadier General Silas Newcomb of Cumberland County was appointed commander of regiments that had

Tea Burners' Monument in Greenwich as it looks today. *Photo by Stephan A. Harrison.*

Potter's Tavern in Bridgeton. *Courtesy of Lummis Research Library.*

been formed of men from the southern counties, including Cumberland. He was stationed in Woodbury. "The difficulty of getting the militia into service became greater as the war was protracted, and the pay became more uncertain and of less value, owing to the depreciation of the Continental currency. These things, combined with the harvest-work and the fear of their own houses being attacked by parties from the British ships during their absence, caused the number in General Newcomb's brigade, who had responded to the call before August 25th [1776] to be less than 300." The two Cumberland County regiments, led by Colonel Elijah Hand and Colonel Potter, numbered eighty-four men.

Colonel Hand's Cumberland County regiment, certainly numbering more men than was reported the previous summer, saved the day (and almost certainly the lives of many Salem County men) when, on March 18, 1778, it double-timed up from Roadstown to Quinton's Bridge. Frank H. Stewart, in his book *Salem County in the Revolution*, recounted what happened:

> *Col. Hand of the Cumberland militia, being informed by Col. Holme* [of the Salem militia], *put his regiment in motion, and was hastening to join Holme at Quinton's bridge, and by an unforeseen Providence, as designed, he arrived there at the very moment when the enemy was dealing out death and destruction among our people. Immediately upon his arrival, he placed his men in the trenches that our* [Salem County] *soldiers had but a little while before left, and opened upon the pursuing enemy such a continued and well directed fire, as soon put a stop to their career and saved our people from being cut to pieces. Hand had with him two pieces of artillery which, when they opened, soon obliged the enemy to face about.*

Three days later, just before dawn, a Loyalist force under the command of Major John G. Simcoe attacked American militiamen headquartered in the Hancock House in Salem County, massacring many men as they slept. The next day, Colonel Charles Mawhood, who commanded the British force then occupying Salem County, issued a proclamation in which he promised to treat kindly the residents of the county and their property if the militia would surrender and give up their arms. If they did not surrender, he promised to reduce them and their families "to beggary and distress." Colonel Hand, commander of the Cumberland County regiment that had saved the day at Quinton's Bridge, replied to Colonel Mawhood's offer and terms:

Interior of Potter's Tavern. *Courtesy of Lummis Research Library.*

Tea Burners' Monument after dedication. *Courtesy of Lummis Research Library.*

It would have given me much pleasure to have found that humanity had been the line of conduct to your troops since you came to Salem. Not only denying quarters, but butchering our men who surrendered themselves prisoners in the skirmish at Quinton's Bridge last Thursday, and bayoneting yesterday morning at Hancock's Bridge in the most cruel manner in cold blood men who were taken by surprise in a situation in which they neither could nor did attempt to make any resistance, and some of whom were not fighting men, are instances too shocking for me to relate and I hope for you to hear.

Your threats to wantonly burn and destroy our houses and other property, and reduce our wives and children to beggary and distress is a sentiment which my humanity almost forbids me only to recite, and induces me to imagine I am reading the cruel order of a barbarous Attila, and not of a Gentleman, brave, generous and polished with a genteel European education.

If Mawhood were to carry out his plan of vengeance, Hand told him, he would only "increase your foes and our army, and retaliation upon Tories and their property is not entirely out of our power. Be assured that these are the sentiments and determined resolution not of myself only but of all the officers and privates under me." Mawhood never carried out his threats.

The British had originally contemplated barging up the Cohansey River to forage in Cumberland County. For reasons unexplained, they changed their mind, went up the Salem River and foraged in Salem County. This, of course, led to the battle at Quinton's Bridge and the massacre at the Hancock House. While they kept out of the Cohansey River, some British landing parties based on ships anchored in Delaware Bay did land on Cumberland soil to forage. Cushing and Sheppard described it: "During the presence of the British fleet in Delaware Bay, parties from them came ashore in search of provisions and plundered the houses of some of the residents near the shore."

According to the historians, most residents of Cumberland County were Whigs or Patriots. However, even though most people were opposed to recent British policies and, of course, British rule by force of arms, they also refused to join the Patriot forces against the government. "Some of these [people held offices] that required them to pledge allegiance to the king and their conscience would not permit them now to take an oath which would require them to oppose him." At one point, the Whig government then in power in the county brought a large number of these people who were against the war into court for refusing to pledge allegiance to the new government of the United States of America. If in court they still refused to pledge allegiance to the new government, many were fined and a few imprisoned.

An interesting case was that of Daniel Bowen. He was the brother of Jonathan Bowen, a prominent Whig in the county and a member of the Provincial Congress. Daniel spoke openly in favor of continuing British rule, and he eventually became an officer in the British army. When the British army was on the verge of being defeated, he, like many other Loyalists, moved to Nova Scotia, where he remained for the rest of his life. However, he maintained a correspondence with his brother and other relatives and friends for many years after the war's end.

Another county resident, Richard Cayford, also became a British officer. Furthermore, he persuaded some friends who were residents of Hopewell Township to also continue their allegiance to the king. At war's end, they all wound up in Nova Scotia, but unlike Daniel Bowen, a number of them returned to Cumberland County.

According to Cushing and Sheppard:

In August, 1777, General Newcomb sent a detachment of militia into Downe [Township] *and arrested fifteen persons, twelve of whom were*

Sheppard homestead and river landing where the brig *Greyhound* delivered tea in 1774. *Courtesy of Lummis Research Library.*

discharged upon taking the oath to the State. The others were convicted of assisting the British and of having instructions how to act if there should be a landing [in the county by British or Loyalist forces]. One Daniel Shaw was their ringleader, and he planned to capture Gen. Newcomb and take him aboard the [British] fleet, and he made efforts to spike the cannon in a redoubt near the Maurice River, but without success.

The only recorded deadly encounter to take place in Cumberland County during the American Revolution occurred in late August 1781. What exactly happened is a little bit unclear. Only a few details are contained in a very brief account of the incident that appeared in an unnamed Philadelphia newspaper. Other reports were supplied sometime after the event by people who were present or who knew those who were present.

The newspaper reported on August 29 that "last week, seven refugees were brought to town." The town referred to is Dallas Landing, which was located just north of present-day Port Norris. Refugees were also known as Tories, people who remained loyal to British authority and the Crown. It is not clear why they were "brought to town" or who or what brought them. The account goes on to report that these refugees, who may have been trying to gain the protection of the British (whose warships were off the coast), attempted to board a "shallop" that was manned by militiamen. Imagine a shallop as a very large rowboat. Again, it is not clear why the refugees boarded the shallop—unless, perhaps, as previously implied, they expected to rendezvous with a British ship in the harbor.

The newspaper account continues: "The Militia were in a shallop, which the refugees attempted to board, when a sharp conflict ensued, during which seven of the Tories were killed and the remaining seven (all wounded) submitted. There were fifteen in all, and it is said that their captain called out that he would give no quarter, which occasioned the action to become desperate."

Another version of the incident was supplied by Thomas Beesley, who was a boy at the time but claimed to have witnessed the encounter. According to young Beesley, Captain James Riggins, who was in charge of the militia detail, killed four or five of the Tories as they tried to board the shallop: "He [Riggins] fired his musket twice and then made such good use of the breech that at the end of the contest there was little left [of the musket] besides the gun barrel. [Militiaman John] Peterson was wounded by one of the refugees, who whereupon was about finishing him by cleaving his head open with a broadsword, when Peterson's son shot the Tory dead. Every refugee was either killed or wounded, some desperately. A boy, the fifteenth member of the group, was the only one to escape unharmed."

One of the last confrontations to take place in the county before the end of the war also involved a shallop. On January 31, 1783, the *Blacksnake*—presumably manned by Tories—was boarded by nineteen militiamen from Downe Township under the command of Captain Low.

Cushing and Sheppard concluded their account of Cumberland County in the American Revolution as follows: "No other county has a brighter record for self-sacrificing patriotism than Cumberland. The ravages of war did not touch her borders, but she was prompt to assist in the defense of the adjoining counties, and her sons fought gallantly from the disastrous battle on Long Island to the glorious consummation of American hopes at Yorktown."

Chapter 5

WHAT'S IN A NAME?

How about the name Elmer, for example. The Elmer family may have given its name to a town in neighboring Salem County, but they made their home and history in Cumberland County and New Jersey, as well as in the brand-new United States of America.

Ebenezer Elmer, at age twenty-two, started making family history on a dark December night in 1774. Like many other residents of the county, he had become incensed at the way Great Britain levied taxes on Americans to support its questionable involvement in world affairs of its own making. Lately, this discontent had focused on Parliament's tax on tea. Massachusetts men about Ebenezer's age had already exercised their discontent by dumping a cargo of tea into Boston Harbor.

Now, on this night in Greenwich, an important inland port on the Cohansey River, a cargo of tea had been offloaded from a ship bound for Philadelphia and stored in the basement of a building belonging to Dan Bowen. Ebenezer and other young men opposed to the tax and disposed toward independence made themselves up to resemble Lenape Indians, hauled the tea out of Bowen's basement and burned it on the town square.

Of course, the "Indians" had violated the law and had to be punished. Chief Justice Frederick Smythe presided at the next court session, which was held the following May in Bridgetown. Guess who was responsible for summoning the jury. None other than Jonathan Elmer, Ebenezer's brother, who happened to be the sheriff for Cumberland County. Not surprisingly, Jonathan summoned a jury of Whigs—men who were generally opposed to then current British policy regarding its American colony. Perhaps not at all coincidentally, the jury foreman was another Whig and another Elmer, Daniel, brother to Ebenezer and Jonathan.

Ebenezer, in his journal, described the foregone conclusion to the trial: "Judge Smith gave very Large Charge to the Grand Jury concerning the time & the burning of the tea the fall before. But the Jury came in without doing anything, & Court broke up."

Sheriff Elmer's term expired in June, and the judge called for a new jury, whose foreman was David Bowen. Historical records do not disclose whether David was related to Dan Bowen, in whose house the tea had been stored. Ebenezer and the other "Indians" presumed that the new jury would not be as sympathetic to their cause as the one put together by Jonathan Elmer. In his journal under the date of September 27, Ebenezer wrote, "Twas expected, as Sheriff Bowen had got a jury of Tories, we should be indicted for burning tea…but they could not make out, but made out a presentment. Court broke up." There was no further attempt to indict and punish the "Indians."

Jonathan, who had graduated from the first medical class at the University of Pennsylvania in 1769 and had "retired" as sheriff in the spring of 1775, was soon thereafter chosen to be the captain of a light infantry company in the Cumberland militia.

As all of this was happening in his life, Jonathan composed what he termed an address to the people of Cumberland County that spring. He said that he had a "few words" to say "on the present situation of public affairs":

America has never seen a more critical period than the present. [His Majesty's government] *has, for a series of years past, assiduously endeavored by every imaginable artifice to enslave us, but the freeborn Colonists who have extended the British Empire over this once savage land with the love of liberty, have resolutely opposed every attack hitherto made to infringe their constitutional rights and privileges.*

The original source of our present disputes is reducible to this single question: Has the parliament of Great Britain a right to tax America internally? It being evident then that the parliament has no right to impose taxes on America, it follows that their claim is no better founded than the robber's who demands my money with a pistol at my breast. We are therefore justified by the fundamental principles of our constitution, by reason, by nature, yea by God himself in opposing with all our might the payment of every such demand. Courage, then, my friends! Let us convince

L.Q.C. Elmer.

the world that Britons will be Britons still in every age & every clime; that we value our Liberties as dearer than our Lives. No nation or people under heaven ever drew the sword in support of a juster or nobler cause than that in which we are now engaged.

In December 1775, Jonathan and Ebenezer Elmer joined with a small group of like-minded men to write and publish the *Plain Dealer*, New Jersey's first newspaper (of a sort). Some historians do not consider the *Plain Dealer* to be a newspaper, per se, because it was not printed. Its few pages were handwritten and left on a table in Potter's Tavern in Bridgetown. The

Plain Dealer was made available in the tavern every Tuesday beginning on December 21, 1775. Its last issue was "published" on February 12, 1776.

The writers stated their position in the first issue: "As the circumstances of the times call on every individual to exert himself for the good of His country and fellow creatures, several persons whose genius and inclination for many years past have led them to study and contemplation, have concluded that the results of their enquiries and speculations on political occurrences and other important subjects [are] particularly calculated to just this place."

In the January issue, the writer lumped Americans into three classes. The first class consisted of those people who adhere to the doctrine of "passive obedience and nonresistance." In the second class were those people who believe that governments must be "at all times accountable to their constituents." The third class, according to the writer, consisted of "great numbers of ignorant, thoughtless beings who are one day Tories and the next day Whigs."

In the fall of 1777, Jonathan was elected to the Continental Congress, serving three terms. He later was elected to the United States Senate and served one term. While remembered chiefly because of his role as champion of American independence, Jonathan was the first New Jersey native to be awarded a medical degree from an American medical school. Dr. Benjamin Rush, the physician made famous because of his role in the American Revolution, once said of Jonathan that "in medical knowledge, he was exceeded by no physician in the United States."

Jonathan's brother, Ebenezer—who later in life was called "Tea Stacks" by close friends and relatives who knew about that night in 1774 when he put on war paint—also played a prominent role in shaping the policies and direction of the new nation. He was a member of the state legislature and served six years in Congress. In the War of 1812, he served as adjutant general of the New Jersey militia and brigadier general of the Cumberland brigade.

The Elmer for whom the Salem County borough is named bore the imposing name Lucius Quintius Cincinnatus, the same as the great Roman statesman. He was the son of Ebenezer and the nephew of Jonathan. He served New Jersey in several capacities, as a member of Congress and as a judge on the state's highest court. He is best known as a distinguished lawyer and jurist rather than as a politician and one-time legislator. Indeed, according to Cushing and Sheppard, "[P]olitics becoming somewhat distasteful for him, he retired from active participation." His retirement might have been encouraged by his having been defeated for reelection.

What's in a Name?

Although he was a prominent and respected member of the New Jersey Supreme Court, Lucius Q.C. may have become best known as the author of *Elmer's History of Cumberland County, New Jersey* (George F. Nixon, publisher, 1869). He turned out to be a very capable historian and a pretty fair storyteller. Here he describes, with more than a hint of sarcasm, a night during the American Revolution when the enemy (British soldiers) were "spotted" approaching Bridgeton:

> *About two o'clock of a midsummer night the gun was fired, and the bell rang with great animation. The scene that ensued may be imagined, but cannot easily be described, and great was the consternation. No one doubted that an enemy was close at hand. One or two persons threw their silver down the well. The militia, except some who as usual were among the missing, were assembled, [and] an attempt [was] made to organize them for action. Happily, however, their prowess was not tested.*
>
> *The alarm, although not sounded until all doubt of its necessity seemed to be removed, turned out to be a false one, originating in the fright of a family near the guard-house, the head of which was absent, and in the fool-hardiness of the skipper of a small sloop, who took it into his head to pass the guard without answering their challenger, and who succeeded in bringing on himself and his crew a volley of musketry, and running the risk of being killed by a ball which passed directly over his head.*

Chapter 6
SHUCKS

C enturies ago, Lenape Indian men pushed offshore in their handmade canoes and into the river and bay named for their tribe—the Delaware. They headed for mudflats. They were looking for oysters. And they found them.

Men under sail and men relying on engine power have been looking for and finding oysters off Cumberland County ever since, though there are not as many today as when Port Norris called itself the "oyster capital of the world" and meant it.

According to the New Jersey Division of Fish and Wildlife, "Descriptions of the oyster beds have been found in writings dating back to 1642, demonstrating the social and economic significance of the resource to early European settlers. Thomas Campanius Holm, an early Swedish settler, wrote in 1642 that Delaware Bay oysters were 'so very large that the meat alone is the size of one of our oysters, shell and all.'"

It didn't take long for the markets that served the East Coast population in the seventeenth and eighteenth centuries to learn about, import and sell the oysters harvested by men sailing down the Maurice and Cohansey Rivers and into the Delaware Bay. Forty years before the American Revolution, sloops and schooners were being built in Cumberland and Salem Counties as quickly as possible to meet the demand of captains and crews bent on harvesting oysters in the bay. "As with many other natural resources of the New World," noted Fish and Wildlife, "the oyster beds were seemingly vast and unending. Often, large quantities of oysters would be thrown into fires

The oyster boat *A.B. Newcomb.*

The oyster boat *A.B. Newcomb* in Delaware Bay, circa 1935.

Oyster boats in their heyday on the Delaware.

in order to produce lime for quick lime. At the time, management of the oyster resource was of little or no concern."

The New Jersey Division of Fish and Wildlife pointed out that starting three hundred years ago, the Delaware Bay seedbeds off the coast of southern New Jersey, particularly Cumberland County, were and still are primary seedbeds for both the seed oyster and the market oyster; however, as we will note in more detail later, the market for oysters is no longer as great or as profitable as it was decades ago. Reported Fish and Wildlife:

> *During the industry's early history, oysters were harvested from the natural beds and sold directly to market. In the mid-1800s, oystermen, concerned with the scarcity of market-sized oysters occurring on the seedbeds, began to plant smaller sized oysters* [presumably smaller than those remembered by Mr. Holm] *that they had formerly sold to areas in the lower bay.*
>
> *By 1856, oyster production shifted from one of direct market from the seed beds to one of replanting and growing oysters in higher salinity waters of the lower bay before being harvested for market. During the previous decade or two, the oystermen had discovered the rewards and advantages of transplanting smaller oysters from the seedbeds into areas of higher*

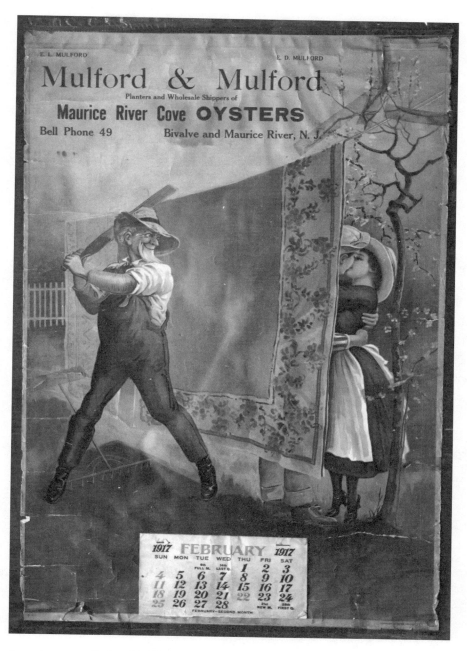

An oyster poster displayed in Bivalve. *Photo by Stephan A. Harrison.*

"Floating" oysters.

Loading barrels of oysters into boxcars. *Collection of the Bayshore Center at Bivalve.*

Bivalve shipping sheds. *Collection of the Bayshore Center at Bivalve.*

salinities. Transplanting small, non-marketable size oysters was a means of mitigating the effects of the declining stocks of large oysters on the natural beds [the ones remembered by Mr. Holm].

Principal oyster planting grounds were off the coast of Cumberland County, primarily the Maurice River Cove. The oyster harvest and marketing were so great and profitable by the latter quarter of the nineteenth century that the Central Railroad Company, with the blessing of the oystermen (many of whom had settled in a booming Port Norris), built railroad tracks into Bivalve in 1876 to allow for the transportation of fresh oysters to waiting markets. In the first year, an average of ten railroad cars loaded with fresh oysters were being shipped out of Bivalve each week to waiting markets up and down the East Coast. By the year 1880, oystermen were shipping out of Bivalve 17,735,000 pounds of oysters valued at $2,080,000. Seven years later, they shipped 23,523,000 pounds of fresh oysters. In the year 1886, the Central Railroad Company was transporting oysters in as many as ninety railroad cars *each week.* Also in that year, more than three hundred dredge boats and three thousand men were engaged in harvesting oysters and preparing them for market.

An early Bivalve street scene. *Collection of the Bayshore Center at Bivalve.*

As the Delaware Bay oyster harvest—most of it credited to crews out of Bivalve—evolved into a major and very profitable industry, the State of New Jersey decided that it had to take steps to regulate the booming industry. According to the National Park Service:

> *In an effort to preserve the limited supply of seedlings in the area, the New Jersey Legislature initiated a series of protective laws. In 1893, the state was divided into seven districts "with a commission of fourteen members to promote the propagation and growth of seed oysters and to protect the natural seed grounds." The legislature empowered the Planters' Association of Maurice River Cove to make rules governing the industry, to employ guards, and to assess fees.*
>
> *In 1899, the State passed yet another bill to enhance the protective stances of the first two bills. Fifteen years later, New Jersey created the Board of Shell Fisheries to further ensure the longevity of the Delaware Bay oyster harvest, which by 1917 had evolved into a $10 million a year industry.*

In September 1910, the *Bridgeton Evening News* reported, rather dramatically, about the planting of oysters in the Maurice River Cove:

On the deck of an oyster schooner. *Collection of the Bayshore Center at Bivalve.*

No human eye looks on the oyster as it grows to maturity, but the Lord watches it until, in due time, fruition appears. Danger lurks, however, in every passing breeze and sudden storm lest the young growth be covered with debris or attacked by the parasites of the deep. Subject to so many dangers, seen and unseen, the oyster planter assumes a greater risk than the farmer who can largely see the visible, whereas the oysterman is in the midst of the uncertainties of the invisible. In the face of all this, the oystermen of Cumberland County have built up the greatest business in southern New Jersey. Great is the magnitude of the Maurice River Cove and Delaware Bay oyster industry.

The newspaper described this "greatest business" in Cumberland County: "There is a yearly average of 350 oyster vessels licensed by the State Oyster Commission. The number of men who stand on the decks of these crafts exceeds 3,000 in all. Wages to the average of $40 a month are paid, so that by the end of the season probably $500,000 in cash is carried to the homes of those who labor on the deck."

The newspaper also reported on how great the investment in and profit from the oyster industry had become by 1910: "The total value of vessels, dredge machinery and other property connected with the proper transaction of this great business comes but little short of $2 million. From September 1, 1909 to June, 1910, the aggregate number of pounds of oysters sent by freight shipment by Central Railroad of New Jersey

Oystermen and their baskets. *Collection of the Bayshore Center at Bivalve.*

and West Jersey and Seashore Railroad from both banks of the Maurice River at Bivalve by bag and barrel was in record figures [of] about $89,000,000."

At one point, it was estimated (though never proven) that there were more millionaires per square mile in the Port Norris area than anywhere else in New Jersey—possibly in the nation. The *Bridgeton Evening News*, in its September 1910 edition, reported that

> *much capital is required to keep the immense business in successful operation. The demand for better vessels and more modern appliances increases from year to year. Keen brains are required to bring success. Many oystermen have acquired wealth during the last twenty years. By dint of personal energy and foresight they have acquired fortunes ranging from $20,000 to $50,000.* [Could the writer, I.T. Nichols, have left off another zero?] *Notable among them are Henry Wallen of Fairton; Miles Gandy of Cedarville; the late Ephraim Mulford of Cedarville, who was a prince among oystermen; Lorenzo G. Donnelly of Heislerville; Howard Socwell, John Lake, and George Robbins of Port Norris; and Peter Cosier of Newport.*

The newspaper article went on to heap praise on the oysters in the bay and the industry responsible for bringing those oysters to tables up and down the coast and beyond. "The Maurice River Cove and Delaware Bay Oysters are the finest in the market. They are the choice bivalves of the leading hotels and cafes of New York, Boston, Philadelphia and other great cities." However, Nichols thought it necessary to criticize Dr. Harvey Washington Wiley, who had been a prime mover for the Food and Drug Act of 1906 and who apparently had gained some national attention for remarks about the oyster industry. Wrote Nichols:

> *Chemical analysis will not deprecate the splendid qualities of our oysters, and no amount of sophistry on the part of Dr. Wiley, national food expert, can destroy it. The magnificent industry of the Maurice River Cove and Delaware Bay is one of the great health assets of the people. It should be fostered and protected by kindly legislation, and every oysterman in Cumberland County can safely depend on the writer* [Mr. Nichols evidently referring to himself] *for intelligent support on whatever position he may be placed to so legislate as to conduce to the enlargement and the general prosperity of not only the owner and captain in command*

This page: Packing oysters. *Collection of the Bayshore Center at Bivalve.*

but the man on the deck upon whose broad shoulders, after all is said, the future of Cumberland County's greatest industry rests.

Unfortunately, the "magnificent industry of the Maurice Cove and Delaware Bay" hit a kind of sinkhole. The year was 1957. According to the Division of Fish and Wildlife, the industry that year

Men shovel oysters in float. *Collection of the Bayshore Center at Bivalve.*

suffered its most serious obstacle. That spring, heavy mortality was discovered in oysters planted the previous year on the New Jersey leased grounds. The cause, soon discovered to be a protozoan parasite, had previously been unknown to the scientific community. It was initially given the acronym MSX, standing for multinucleated sphere unknown…By the end of 1959, 90–95% of the oysters on the planted grounds, and about half of those on the seedbeds, had died. Total harvest in the Delaware Bay fell from 711,000 bushels in 1956 to only 49,000 bushels in 1960.

Fortunately, the oysters developed a natural resistance to MSX, and by the late 1970s and early 1980s, as many as one hundred large oyster boats were being built each year in New Jersey to dredge seed oysters. Then, just as things were looking up, disaster struck again. According to Fish and Wildlife, "In 1985, after 15 years of modest prosperity, the oyster industry in the Delaware Bay suffered another setback, a resurgence of MSX disease accompanied a period of severe drought. High mortalities affected planted and seed oysters until 1987, when the conditions on the beds began to modestly improve." During the harvest season of 1990, 160,000 bushels of seed oysters were transplanted, and the next year, 290,000 bushels of oysters were harvested, considered the best yield in more than ten years.

It seemed that for every recovery, the industry suffered a setback. In the 1990s, the oyster beds were struck by a disease called Dermo. The result was heavy losses of both planted and seed oysters, and the industry went into rather severe decline. By the new century, the twenty-first, the industry in Bivalve had been significantly reduced. "Today," Fish and Wildlife reported in 2002, "there is currently one shucking house and one packing house, with combined employment of about 50, operating in the town of Bivalve... Because of the decline in oyster production from the Delaware Bay, they process mostly out-of-state oysters, especially from Connecticut."

Again, however, just as the oyster industry declines off the Delaware Bay coast in Cumberland County and many people connected with it give up hope, there are some people who still look to the future and feel confident that it will be better. "The native Delaware Bay oyster," reported Fish and Wildlife, "over a period of time and through natural selection, has apparently developed a resistance to MSX. Today, oystermen, managers and scientists are hopeful that the oysters are again on their way to recovery."

"OLD-TIMERS RECALL OYSTER BOATS"

On October 23, 1999, the *News of Cumberland County* printed an article by staff writer Jean Jones with this title. One of the "old-timers" was Arthur Hinson, who remembered being out in the oyster boat for up to two weeks at a time. "'The purpose of not going in,' he said, 'was that you wouldn't have a crew. They'd go off and get drunk and wouldn't come back.'" Other "old-timers" interviewed by Ms. Jones included John DuBois and Bill Biggs. "Hinson said a lot of men got their legs broken on the boats. DuBois remembered a captain who got caught in the rigging for the sails and a puff of wind pulled him out over the river. 'We pulled him in and he never even got wet.'"

She continued:

> *Asked about the size of the crews, the men said a small boat might have four men, a captain and a cook, while the bigger boats might have 16 or 18 men.*
>
> *"Shell Pile and Bivalve and Mauricetown were pretty big towns,"* *DuBois said. Each shanty would have six, eight, 10 people living there.*

George Lemuth, lab assistant, studies oysters. *Collection of the Bayshore Center at Bivalve.*

They had a pretty good income between them. If somebody didn't pay the rent, the landlord would take off the door. "You'd go by and there would be bags hanging over the doors, and the people were still there."

Life along the Delaware Bay could be rough in the fall and winter when icy decks on the oyster boats were a constant hazard to the crew, many of whom never learned to swim. "In the early days, they didn't have a pilot house," said Hinson. "They would spread ashes from the cook stove on the deck so the men wouldn't slip." DuBois recalled that the coffee was made in the morning, and the pot was never emptied, just added to.

The oystermen, like those interviewed by Ms. Jones, still drink their morning coffee and then go out in search of oysters. However, there simply are not as many men, and they don't find as many oysters as they used to.

Chapter 7

"THEY MAKE GLASS"

The principal ingredient needed for making glass is silica (sand), and Cumberland County in the eighteenth and nineteenth centuries had as much as any county in New Jersey and more than most counties in America. The county also was heavily forested, and that meant wood for the fires needed to turn silica into glass.

So there were acres and square miles of sand and wood in the late 1700s in Cumberland County. So what? James Lee is what. Lee, who came to the brand-new United States of America from Ireland as a very young man, arrived in Port Elizabeth from Philadelphia in 1797. He was twenty-six years old, and America was twenty-one years old. The historian Lucius Q.C. Elmer described the upstart as "an active, enterprising man, too spasmodic in his efforts to succeed well." Elmer was only half right.

It is not certain how much the young enterpriser from Philadelphia knew about glassmaking, if anything, but he made two smart decisions. The first was to ask his brother still living in Philadelphia to put up enough money so that together they could purchase one thousand or more acres of pine and oak trees from the very wealthy widow Elizabeth Bodley, for whom Port Elizabeth was named. The second smart decision was to make friends with the Stanger family. The Stanger brothers, all seven of them, had come from Germany and knew something—enough at least—about making window glass. Indeed, some members of the Stanger family were already at work making glass for the Wistar family in Salem County.

A 1938 aerial view of Lower Glassworks in Millville.

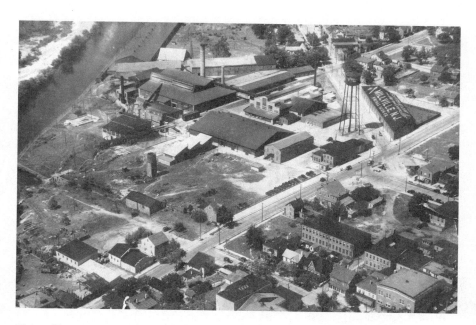

Upper Glassworks in Millville, circa 1938.

Andrew Bennett at Whithall Tatum factory.

It is not certain exactly when or why the glassmaking business founded by Lee and the Stanger families in 1799 was first called the Eagle Glass Works. It may be that the name was derived from the new nation's symbolic bird. In any event, in the year 1806, when Christian Stanger purchased a tract of land from the Lee brothers, the deed made reference to the "Maurice River Glass Works." By any other name, this was the first glasshouse in Cumberland County, the third one in New Jersey and one of very few in America.

The Stanger family, no less enterprising than the Lee brothers, built a hotel in Port Elizabeth in 1807. They called it the Rising Sun. The family also started to make more than window glass. According to Adeline Pepper in her book *Glass Gaffers of New Jersey*, while the Eagle Glass Works started by making window glass, "who can doubt, considering the needs of the local hotel, the neighboring industries and the potential trade in the West Indies, that much other glass was made here, especially bottles and tableware. The Stangers were particularly noted for their expert bottle making."

The young, enterprising James Lee and his brother sold part of their interest in the business to a group of investors in 1810, and the restless James moved on to Millville, where he got in on the ground floor of glassmaking there, and then, perhaps becoming a little "spasmodic," he relocated to the western frontier. James sold the remainder of his interest in Eagle Glass Works in 1815. According to the *Vineland Historical Magazine*, he offered to sell his part ownership through an ad in the *Aurora*, a Philadelphia newspaper: "One quarter part of the whole, or $7,000 stock in the Eagle Glass Works at Port Elizabeth. These works are in full operation and in as high repute as any cylinder glass works in the United States." Lee also was selling land he owned that supported the Eagle Glass Works. The ad mentioned the availability of 2,900 acres "containing a fine growth of pine and oak timber worth $1.25 a cord."

At about the same time, two of the Stanger brothers, Jacob and Frederick, along with William Shough, started the Union Glass Works in Port Elizabeth. In 1811, according to Ms. Pepper, "[T]he 8-pot furnace went into blast, with the original three partners as managers and blowers and also Solomon, Phillip and Francis Stanger, and Daniel Focer and Daniel Shough as blowers. Medicine vials were the main items blown…In December 1811, the building burned to the ground. It was not rebuilt until 1812 and did not go into blast until March of that year." For whatever reason—and the most informed guess is that the partners had a parting of the ways—the Union Glass Works shut down its furnaces for good in 1818.

As was previously noted, James Lee, the industrious Irishman, moved on to Millville, where he founded what became known as Glasstown on

Flint glass factories in south Millville.

the east bank of the Maurice River in the first decade of the nineteenth century. The location of this first glass manufacturing plant in Millville is now the site of American Legion Post No. 82 at the intersection of Buck and Mulberry Streets.

The original plant, which produced tableware, bottles and window glass, was sold by Lee in 1814 to Gideon Scull. After Scull, who produced only holloware, the business changed hands a number of times before finally being sold again in 1838. The principal new owner was a former sea captain by the name of John M. Whitall. He knew next to nothing about making glass, but he was smart enough to rely on those who were experts, and he was sufficiently wealthy to invest enough money in the business to help make Millville a major center of glassmaking in New Jersey and America for more than a century.

In her book about glassmaking in New Jersey, Ms. Pepper wrote that while James Lee relied on his brother's money to help support the glassmaking business in Port Elizabeth, John Whitall leaned on his brother, Franklin, who had a "good business education." In 1848, Edward Tatum joined the Whitalls. Both the Whitalls and Tatums, according to Ms. Pepper, were devout Quakers. "So faithful were the Tatums that when they were not at home, the story goes, their horses trotted alone to the meeting house."

In 1857, the firm changed its name to Whitall Tatum Company and was incorporated under that title in 1901. "Even before incorporation," wrote Ms. Pepper, "the glass company had become a giant...and famed for the extraordinary high quality of its moldblown ware."

Of course, Whitall Tatum Company was not alone in the glassmaking industry. Indeed, Lewis Mulford and associates were operating a glassmaking business south of Millville at about the time that the company name Whitall Tatum was attached to the business in Millville. Sales were not good for Mulford's factory in the mid-1850s, and he offered to sell the company to Whitall Tatum. The larger, more successful business in Millville declined the offer. Ms. Pepper related what happened next: "In retaliation, Mulford cornered all wood for miles around. In a counter-move, Whitall Tatum began buying wood from Virginia and shipping it by boat. With this slow and unreliable transport, they found themselves frequently running out of fuel. In the end, they had no choice but to capitulate and buy [Mulford's business.]" Of course, the biggest glassmaking business in Cumberland County just got bigger.

Armstrong Cork Corporation purchased Whitall Tatum in 1938, but in the decades since the showdown with Mulford, the company produced many of the bottles, jars and vials used by families growing up in the still-

Men working at Mitchell Glass Company in Millville. *Courtesy of Steelman Photographics.*

growing America. Pharmacies, in particular, began using bottles produced by Whitall Tatum for prescriptions, other chemicals and perfumes. Also, the company introduced such innovations in glass manufacturing as new formulas for making glass and wood casts that allowed glass to be molded without showing a casting line.

In 1999, after almost two hundred years of glass production, the old Whitall Tatum factory was closed.

While Whitall Tatum was still at its peak, the growing demand for glass products in post–Civil War America was at its peak, and glass industries began to multiply—particularly, of course, in silica-rich southern New Jersey and Cumberland County. Dr. Theodore Wheaton, a physician who opened a pharmacy in Millville in 1883, probably was one of Whitall Tatum's better customers. While a physician by training, he also was a smart businessman, and the glassmaking industry was booming. Five years after opening his pharmacy, Wheaton started making glass bottles and tubing at a plant that employed thirty-six people working a six-pot furnace. Almost eighty years later, in 1966, the Wheaton Glass Company was a prominent fixture in the glassmaking industry.

By the way, as an indication of how the glassmaking industry boomed and prospered after the Civil War, particularly in Cumberland County, the city of Bridgeton in the last decades of the nineteenth century boasted (if that's the right word) twenty glassmaking industries. Most of them were fairly small operations, but in the twentieth century, the Owens-Illinois Glass Company became the largest glassworks in the area, employing as many as 2,500 people working at eight furnaces by the middle decades.

Early in that century, a student at Knox College in Illinois, not unlike other young men at the time, traveled the country one summer vacation by "riding the rails," often sneaking aboard freight cars like a hobo. He found his way to Millville, and the trip prompted him to write about his experience. Here is an excerpt from his essay:

> *Down in southern New Jersey, they make glass. By day and by night, the fires burn on in Millville and bid the sand let in the light. The glassblowers union is one of the most perfect organizations in the country. Passing back and forth in the pale weird light, these creatures are imps in both the modern and oldtime sense of the word. Their education has consisted mainly of the thoughts, emotions and experiences that resulted from contact with "blowers" and "gaffers," besides views of a big barn-like space lit up by white hot sand. In the use of the ever surviving if not ever fitting superlative, "damndest," they are past masters all.*

The young college student from Illinois was Carl Sandburg.

Chapter 8

PAINTING A NEW GOLDEN AGE

U nfortunately, it was a familiar chain of events that had already locked other cities into a time period that no longer existed. The twentieth century was drawing to a close, but downtown Millville was still stuck in its middle decades. An article by Jacqueline L. Urgo in the *Philadelphia Inquirer* described what had happened:

> *High Street's last golden age came toward the end of the 19th century, when industrialist money that had spun indigenous sand into highly prized glass helped build turreted and stone-carved buildings along a bustling street. Decline began in the 1960s when plastics trumped glass as king and thousands lost their jobs in the handful of glass mills that were left in the town. Empty storefronts began to appear like ugly cavities along the once-bright [High Street]. A nearby mall pulled away whatever business had been left.*

Liz Nicklus, interim director of the new Riverfront Renaissance Center for the Arts on today's High Street, put it plainly: "We had a downtown here [in the last decades of the twentieth century] that was practically abandoned. You'll hear people say differently, but we have the facts. High Street [business establishments] were half empty in the late 1990s. People who had moved to [the suburbs] would tell me they hadn't come downtown in ten years because there was nothing to come downtown for."

As the twentieth century was nearing its end, so was Millville's business district. According to James Quinn, former mayor of Millville and now

Kim Ayres is director of planning and community development for Millville. *Photo by Stephan A. Harrison.*

city commissioner and director of public affairs, by the early 1990s the city had lost nearly ten thousand jobs as the glass industry and other related industries expired. "Occupancy rates of storefronts along High Street, our main business district, were less than 50 percent when I took office [as mayor] in 1997."

Unfortunately, for many American cities the size of Millville and larger, those kinds of statistics have resulted in a final decline from which they have never fully recovered. The so-called movers and shakers in those cities apparently forgot how to shake things up and move forward. Fortunately for Millville, Cumberland County and South Jersey, the movers and shakers in and around the city knew what had to be done and did it.

The so-called renaissance for downtown Millville perhaps began when very bright and forward-thinking individuals got together in the 1990s and reminded one another that Wheaton Arts on the outskirts of the city already drew large crowds to its site to learn about the once-famous glassworks of Millville and to view displays of exquisite glassware. These individuals, united as the Millville Development Corporation, decided that perhaps people also might be attracted to the work of artists other than just those who worked with glass. As a result of their decision, a letter bearing the

Wheaton Village letterhead was sent in November 1998 to artists and others soliciting their interest in the creation of an arts district in Millville.

The letter, signed by Barry Taylor as president of Wheaton Village, advised recipients that Millville was

> conducting a feasibility study to assess the creation of a downtown arts district in the city. Its traditional "main street" is being revitalized through a series of public and private initiatives, and is well on its way to its goals. Millville has attracted a small but growing number of artists and craftspeople. The plan is to develop cultural tourism while maintaining its small town ambiance and traditions. It is prepared to work with artists, Wheaton Village and other corporate and public partners to develop an arts district with the facilities and support needed by artists.

The following July, a flyer went out to a number of artists and artisans inviting them to an open meeting at the Millville Library "to help establish a gallery in a planned arts district on High Street. The gallery would offer space for exhibitions, studios, classes—you name it! We would get *terrific* exposure for our work. The possibilities are endless."

According to Kim Ayres, director of planning and community development for the newly created Glasstown Arts District, the planners of the meeting at the library hoped to attract twenty-five people who might share their desire and commitment. As it turned out, more than one hundred artists and artisans attended. "That was the turning point. That's when we realized we could do this. Also, fortunately, we had and still have very progressive minded city leaders. They never limited us. As long as we could supply some evidence that this [arts district] could work, they were willing to try it."

The Riverfront Renaissance Center for the Arts opened in April 2001 in a building that had once housed a men's and boys' clothing store. It was just the beginning of the renaissance. Jacqueline L. Urgo, writing in the *Philadelphia Inquirer* in November 2002, reported that "along High Street, the boards are coming down. Six new businesses have opened in the district, and about a dozen more—including an arts supply store, two restaurants and a jazz club—are planned for the coming year." Writing about the Center for the Arts, she described how $500,000 had been invested to convert the old clothing store. "The Center houses a gallery—with exhibitions that change monthly, studio space for artists; and an education gallery where budding artisans can learn crafts and about marketing their wares."

A jazz band performs in Millville's Levoy Theatre in the early 1900s.

Levoy Theatre in Millville, circa 1930. *Courtesy of Steelman Photographics.*

The public's response to the new Glasstown Center Arts District has been "fabulous," according to Liz Nicklus. "You know, people always thought that Millville was just a place where they made glass, that there was nothing here except the glass industry, which, of course, is now gone. We decided we wanted people to walk [down High Street] and be surprised, to see art that they never thought they'd see in Millville."

Nicklus said the Glasstown Arts District has attracted artists from all over the country. "There's always something for everybody. It could be something conventional one month and then something off the wall the following month. We give artists a chance to show their work who normally would not have the chance to display their work."

At the start of 2012, the Glasstown Arts District published a report on the current status of the district and what had transpired during the period beginning with the year 2000 and ending December 2011. Over those years, according to the report, eighty-one new businesses were created, and another twenty-eight expanded. While Millville probably will never come close to re-creating the thousands of jobs lost when glassmaking and other industries folded years ago, the district report noted that during the eleven years, 385 jobs had been created. Insofar as public and private investment in the reinvention of downtown Millville is concerned, the report stated that, for the period, private investment in "purchased and new property construction" totaled $14,417,250. Private investment for building rehabilitation during the same period totaled just over $24 million. As far as public investment during the same period, slightly more than $6 million was contributed.

One of the casualties of Millville's long decline in the last half of the twentieth century was the Levoy Theatre on High Street. It opened in 1908 and showed silent movies. In 1912, it became a vaudeville theater and featured acts making the circuit. By the 1930s, it was the premier showcase for all that Hollywood could produce. In the last half of the century, however, the Levoy, like many downtown theaters, began losing its audience to newer movie theaters included in highway malls. It closed in 1976. The Levoy Theatre, which underwent a multimillion-dollar restoration, was scheduled for a grand reopening as a playhouse in the summer of 2012, a century after it first hosted vaudeville acts on its stage.

Inquirer writer Jacqueline Urgo ended her 2002 article on the rebirth of Millville by quoting Morel Pagano, a watercolorist: "When I came here in 1961, [Millville] was a cultural desert, a cultural wasteland. To see this [the new Glasstown District] happening in this town is incredible. I can't wait to see what happens next." Of course, it's still happening.

Chapter 9

SEABROOK FARMS

The Century-Old Giant

The headline on page one in the July 18, 1913 issue of *Dollar Weekly* read, "C.F. Seabrook, Who Heretofore Managed the Affairs and Operations of A.P. Seabrook & Son, Is the President and General Manager of Seabrook Farms Company." Only three months later, in October, the front page of *Dollar Weekly* featured another headline: "Cumberland's Show Place: The Great Agricultural Operation of Seabrook Farm; Two Hundred Seventy-five Acres, Carloads Shipped to Many Points."

The readers of *Dollar Weekly* and, more importantly, the consumers of farm products around the world would learn to rely on that "Great Agricultural Operation" for another century.

In 1955, *Life* magazine labeled Seabrook Farms the "greatest vegetable factory on earth." By that time, according to the magazine, "with the mass production adeptness usually associated with motor cars, Seabrook Farms last year [1954] grew, gathered and froze 100 million pounds of 29 vegetables and fruits. Its packaged output of lima beans would have stretched 2,250 miles. Often less than an hour elapses from the time a bean is picked until it has been washed, sorted, hand-checked, packaged and quick frozen. Such high-powered activity last year employed 3,200 full-time and part-time workers."

At about the same time that *Life* published its spread on Seabrook Farms, the trade publication *Quick Frozen Foods* printed a forty-page special section about the company. "In addition to growing and processing the crops from its own 19,000 acres," the section read, "Seabrook Farms absorbs the

James M. Seabrook Jr., president of Seabrook Brothers & Sons, checks out the company's food processing line. *Photo by Stephan A. Harrison.*

production of 35,000 acres owned by 1,169 neighboring contract farms. This vast agricultural domain, 54,000 acres of scientifically cultivated soil, spreads across several counties of Southern New Jersey into Delaware, Maryland and Pennsylvania." Echoing *Life*'s headline, the magazine called the Seabrook processing plant the "biggest in the world."

Not only was Seabrook Farms the "greatest vegetable factory on Earth," but it was also a pioneer in frozen foods. John Seabrook, one of C.F.'s three sons (Belford and Courtney were the other two), in writing about the company in 1995, described how Seabrook Farms began freezing its products:

> *Belford had visited Clarence Birds's laboratory in Gloucester, Massachusetts during the summer of 1929 after his freshman year in Princeton. In the summer of 1930, he used direct expansion ammonia in a crude freezer for quick-freezing 20,000 pounds of lima beans, our first experimental venture in this new method of vegetable preservation. The ammonia came from the ice plant C.F. had built during World War I for icing rail cars. Birdseye and Seabrook were a perfect match. General Foods* [which had purchased the Birdseye process] *had patents, capital and marketing know-how. The old varieties of vegetables used for the fresh market or canning were*

Charles F. Seabrook on his father's farm, circa 1913. *Courtesy of Lummis Research Library.*

not suitable for freezing, but Seabrook Farms knew how to quickly develop and use new varieties in commercial quantity. Seabrook Farms also had the land, the know-how, the management skills, a processing plant, and complete control of the entire process from seed to package.

In its 1955 article about Seabrook Farms, *Life* magazine made reference to 3,200 employees. However, the article did not point out that perhaps a majority of that workforce consisted of Japanese Americans who had been recruited from World War II internment camps located in the western states, as well as hundreds of European men and women who had been displaced from their homes by that same war.

As I wrote in my book *Growing a Global Village*, "Looking back at those times when people from the four corners of America and from both hemispheres of the world worked and lived together, the men and women who were there in the global village as children or young adults marvel at how it all came about—how their parents and grandparents made Seabrook Farms the greatest and the best."

Fast-forward to today, a century after C.F. created the Seabrook Farms Company. In 2013, the company is called Seabrook Brothers & Sons and is located off Finley Road in the town of Seabrook. The name of the company has changed a little, but the business has changed significantly.

"The volume of vegetables processed is actually pretty much the same as it was," James M. Seabrook Jr., president of the new/old company and grandson of Belford told me. "Seabrook Farms processed close to a hundred million pounds of frozen vegetables, but they used perhaps as many as 5,000 people. We process about the same but employ about 500 persons." The big difference, he said, is that today most vegetables are planted, harvested and processed by machine. Cumberland and Salem County farmers still grow about half the vegetables frozen by Seabrook, but the company also buys vegetables from farmers in adjoining states; green beans may come from Florida, and broccoli may come from Maine. "Because we're on the Interstate 95 corridor," said Seabrook, "we can go north and south for vegetables."

Seabrook Brothers & Sons freezes and sells about twenty-five vegetables. "The largest crop that we freeze is spinach," said Seabrook, "and a lot of the spinach still comes from right around here in Cumberland County. Our second-biggest crop is green beans, and our third-biggest is peas." Annual income from the sale of 150 million pounds of twenty-five frozen vegetables is about $100 million, said Seabrook.

While the planting and growing of crops has changed little, processing and packaging have changed significantly, continued Seabrook. "In the plant, for example, we use about one quarter of the water and less electricity. We're just more efficient." Insofar as the changes in packaging, Seabrook pointed out that while cartons were used in the past, today vegetables are packaged in plastic bags. Packaging in plastic bags as opposed to cartons reduces the cost by almost half, he added. Another important change is that solar panels now account for one-third of the energy used by the company's facilities. The marketplace is also very different than it was. For example, the biggest customer by far for the frozen products sold by Seabrook Brothers & Sons is Walmart.

Looking back on a century-long connection between the Seabrook family and Cumberland County and New Jersey, James Seabrook could rightfully boast, "We're still helping to keep the garden in the Garden State."

Chapter 10

"WANTED: EVERYONE!"

I n the mid-1930s, Charles F. Seabrook, owner of Seabrook Farms, ran an ad in his company's newsletter, the *Seabrooker*, with this heading in large, boldface type: "**Wanted!**" The ad began as follows: "Wanted men and women who prefer life and work here in the open air, with a home only a few minutes from their work, instead of the shorter hours (and long travel back and forth!) and high wages (and still higher cost of living) in the City. No sulkers or people with touchy feelings need apply." The ad promised a ten-hour day. "However, the work consists in doing whatever the employer feels like asking at any minute of the day or night."

Over the next five decades, thousands of men and women from almost everywhere in the United States, Europe, Central America and the islands of the Caribbean came to work for Mr. Seabrook at his Seabrook Farms. And many (perhaps most) of them stayed, put down permanent roots and raised a family. Descendants of many of those families continue to live and work in Cumberland County.

In the summer of 2012, the *Philadelphia Inquirer* reported:

> *Last month, in its first population estimate since the 2010 count, the U.S. Census Bureau added Cumberland to the list of counties it classifies as "majority minority." Spurred by Latino, African American, and Asian growth in the Vineland-Bridgeton-Millville triangle, Cumberland reached 50.1 percent minority last year, joining 348 other counties—11 percent of the nation's 3,143—whose populations had already passed the same*

Jose Melendez, executive director of Casa PRAC. *Photo by Stephan A. Harrison.*

marker. Latinos, many of whom came to Cumberland County for jobs in agriculture and manufacturing, have driven the county's entry into the majority-minority ranks.

C.F. Seabrook's company, which *Life* magazine once called the "greatest vegetable factory on earth," actively recruited, particularly during the 1940s and 1950s, men and women from the European nations recently liberated from Nazi occupation, Japanese Americans recently liberated from U.S. detention camps and men and women from Puerto Rico and Jamaica.

In my 2003 book *Growing a Global Village: Making History at Seabrook Farms*, I wrote:

> *The term multiculturalism didn't enter the American lexicon until late in the Twentieth Century, but in the middle of the century multiculturalism was outside the front door in the global village* [where Seabrook Farms workers lived]. *"When I was growing up in Seabrook, I used to marvel, because you would go outside and there would be kids talking in Japanese to a kid who was talking in German and another one who was speaking*

Spanish, and they all seemed to understand what they were saying." Fusaye Kazaoka was fourteen when her family came to Seabrook.

The encounters between people of different cultures, languages and races were, of course, common everyday occurrences and almost always welcomed rather than avoided. Again, from my book: "Ingrid Hawk, who, with her parents, walked off the troop ship *John Muir* in New York in 1952 at age four, also had never seen a black person before coming to Seabrook Farms from Germany. But it didn't matter. 'So, there's a person that's black, or there's a person who has eyes different from me. It didn't dawn on me until I was an adult that life at Seabrook Farms was something unique.'"

Of course, while Ingrid Hawk had never seen a black person before coming to this country and knew next to nothing about the history of blacks in America, the people of Cumberland County, like residents of other counties in the early centuries of this nation, knew about blacks and slavery firsthand. In an article published for the county's 250th anniversary, Eileen Bennett of *The Press* of Atlantic City quoted Giles R. Wright, director of Afro-American Studies at the New Jersey Historical Commission: "In Cumberland County, slaves were used in agriculture, working on the large expanses of farmland or tending livestock. In communities that were located near waterways, slaves could be used to go out in ships, catch whales…a wide range of occupations. A third area in which slaves were used was for domestic work. It's hard to imagine any craft or trade in which you wouldn't find black workers."

Ms. Bennett wrote that although slavery existed in Cumberland County, it was nearly at an end by the start of the American Civil War, and when that war was over, there were no more slaves. During the late eighteenth and early nineteenth centuries, an area known as Springtown in Greenwich Township was home to many former slaves, some of whom came to the area from Southern states by way of the Underground Railroad. Indeed, of the seven "station masters" of the Underground Railroad in Cumberland County, five were African Americans living in Springtown.

While slavery has long been absent in Cumberland County, the influx of so-called minorities has been extensive and intensive ever since, particularly since the middle of the twentieth century, as already alluded and attested to by the 2010 census. For more than thirty years, Casa PRAC (Puerto Rican Action Committee) in Vineland has been assisting newly arrived families from Puerto Rico and elsewhere to find housing and jobs and has provided badly needed social services.

Charles Lloyd of the U.S. Colored Volunteer Army, taken during the Civil War. *Courtesy of Lummis Research Library.*

In more recent times, most of the newcomers have come from Mexico, according to Jose A. Melendez, executive director of Casa PRAC, and many are undocumented. Because they are undocumented, said Melendez, "neither the federal government nor do we really know how many Mexicans have come into Cumberland County. The majority of families who migrated from Mexico have settled in Bridgeton."

While most of the men and women who came from Puerto Rico and foreign countries to Cumberland County in the last half of the twentieth century had jobs waiting for them at or through Seabrook Farms, there are many fewer jobs in agriculture today. What jobs, then, await this latest influx of families from Mexico and elsewhere? "A number of persons find work in landscaping and construction," said Melendez. "Some of those persons who started working for landscapers now own their own landscaping business." The fact that many families from Mexico are undocumented makes it difficult for Casa PRAC to provide services for them, said Harold J. Gonzalez, president of the board for Casa PRAC. "Unfortunately, there are some of our programs for which they don't qualify."

Maria LaBoy, who runs Hispanics Pro Educacion in Vineland, was quoted in the *Philadelphia Inquirer* article as seeing "two dimensions to the minority surge. On the positive side, there is a whole new world right in front of you. Your children do not have to leave the county to learn about other cultures and languages. Or, you can look at it negatively, confronting the new people in an accusatory manner." The newspaper's article concluded, "Whether viewed as a net plus or a challenge for the county's limited resources, the changes in Cumberland County are entrenched."

If past history teaches any lessons, the county will most likely find a positive way to address this latest surge from outside its borders.

Chapter 11

HISTORY RECLAIMED

I t is not at all certain why Amaziah Burcham, who had helped to preserve the Union, decided in 1869 to dig up his roots in East Lyme—close by the Connecticut River and the small streams that drain into the Atlantic Ocean—and then travel southwest to replant those roots in the place where the Menantico Creek empties into the Maurice River. But he did, and the Burcham acreage eventually ballooned to almost one hundred acres.

According to the National Park Service, "On the southeastern corner of the land, Burcham built either a frame house or moved into an already existing structure. This location, being the highest point on the property, ensured that, if breaches ever occurred in the dike, the house would remain dry. The floor plan of the original house is unknown due to a number of changes that occurred throughout the Nineteenth Century."

According to researcher Patricia Bovers Ball, "The earliest identified farmhouse building on the Burcham property was a one-room, hall-plan structure that stood at the north end of the existing house. Its small size and pitched roof suggest an 18th century date of construction." Bovers Ball believes that that new sections were added to this original structure until 1961, when it was demolished.

In 1907, Burcham built a brick house on the property as a gift to his newlywed son, Frank, and his wife. According to the National Park Service, "The house was constructed from bricks fired on the premises, adding on to the original structure. The bricks [were] laid in a seven course common bond. Some of the other features of the house include a high pitched roof

An aerial view of Burcham Island in the Maurice River. *Courtesy of Steelman Photographics.*

with a cross gable that faces the Maurice River, an L-shaped porch that wraps around the front, supported by turned supports, and three exterior chimneys, one on the east gable and two on each side of the north gable." The house is still a prominent structure on the property, and because of its location on high ground, it is very visible from the Maurice River.

Of course, Amaziah Burcham didn't come all the way from Connecticut and choose the land where the Menantico Creek empties into the Maurice River because the location was picturesque. After all, he had to make a living. In the late decades of the nineteenth century and first decades of the twentieth century, many houses and business establishments were built with brick, and Burcham discovered that his property was loaded with Cape May clay, which was a gritty and sandy kind of clay very suitable for making bricks, as well as drain tiles. Drain tiles were important for buildings along the rivers and streams.

Burcham figured, of course, that if he needed bricks and tiles for projects on his property, other residents of the area would also need bricks and tiles from time to time. Being a smart man, he put two and two together and came up with one very good idea: the South Jersey Brick and Drain Tile Works.

According to the National Park Service, the South Jersey Brick and Drain Tile Works lasted almost to the end of World War II, and for all that time, brickmaking "was the main economic thrust of the family enterprise; farming was a secondary venture that supplied Burcham's family, employees and animals with food."

Research journalist Debra A. Barsotti described what it was like working for the South Jersey Brick and Drain Tile Works:

> *In the morning, workers would "dig the clay" and fill coal cars.* [Then] *a boiler-powered cable line pulled the coal car over the pit* [and] *the clay was dumped. The cart returned by gravity to the clay pits. After grounding the clay, it was packed into moulds to be shaped. Lengths of bricks were cut by a wire—eight to a pallet* [and] *five pallets high, which were sent to the drying shed. There were three grades of brick: commons, red hards and salmons. Once dried thoroughly, the bricks were wheeled up to the kiln, where the wood-fed "fire box" was burning round the clock during the production period. At the height of the Burcham's brick operation, 15,000 bricks were produced weekly. Horse-drawn wagons carried the final product to buyers, except on one occasion when a barge carried away one load. That one shipment carried 70,000 bricks. The deal was not handled satisfactorily, and no further shipments* [of that size] *left on that barge.*

However, most of the bricks produced at the plant were bought and used by customers living in the Millville area, and often those bricks were loaded onto smaller barges that were pulled up the Maurice River to Millville by horses walking along the dikes. Later, up until the company ceased operations, bricks were hauled by truck.

More than a decade before Amaziah became a Civil War veteran, moved to the east bank of the Maurice River and discovered clay in his backyard, a New Jersey geologist by the name of George Cook suggested in his annual report that banking and draining the tidal marshes on the rivers of southern New Jersey—the Maurice and Cohansey included and in particular—should be expanded. "Cook explained that salt-marsh farmers improved their property by ditching, clearing off coarse hassocks, and opening pods and salt holes to tidal action," reported the National Park Service. "Landowners shut out the tides by building embankments and draining the land via sluices. Once drained to the low-water mark, the agricultural and general value of the land increased." Cook said that the banks already constructed in Cumberland County on the Cohansey River ranged from three to seven feet high and were built directly on the surface of the meadow. Many farmers, the report noted,

> *left one rod or sixteen and a half feet of meadow between the river and the bank to act as a guard or shore, which protected the banks from extremely high tides and gave the workers a reason to make repairs.*
>
> *The cost of building such banks varied according to location. Farmers paid $2 a linear rod to reclaim the area along the Maurice River* [that included the Burcham property]. *This included construction of the banks as well as the cutting of drains and water courses. Along* [the Maurice River] *the ditches were cut to be seven feet wide and two feet deep. Cook reiterated the fact that the best way to keep areas clear was by using wide drains with sloping sides.*

Near the close of the nineteenth century, Cornelius Clarkson Vermeule, an assistant geologist for New Jersey, surveyed what had happened to water supply, flow and power as a result of bank building along the rivers. At the time of his examination, many, if not most, properties along the Maurice River, including the Burcham farm, had been embanked and cultivated. In his report, Vermeule noted that the improvements in building up banks "was very profitable and that the possession of a proper amount of improved meadow would add from 50 percent to 100 percent to the value of neighboring farms, as they afford excellent grazing, enabling the farmers to keep cattle, which is almost impossible to do profitably on the uplands."

Maintaining the river dikes has always been a concern for the Burchams, as well as for other farmers living along the Maurice and Cohansey Rivers. Beginning in the 1950s, the twin sisters Janice and Jeanette inherited the Burcham farm from their father, Frank, and then the riverbanks and the farm and homestead that the banks protected became their concern.

Neither sister would have claimed to be a farmer. Janice was a nurse with the U.S. Navy, and Jeanette had been a schoolteacher and transportation lawyer. However, both women knew the importance of maintaining the dike and farmland. When they first took over the Burcham farm, the sisters used river mud and pieces of brick left from the days of the old Brick and Tile Drain Works to maintain their property's dikes. They and some other farmers along the Maurice River finally hired a "muddigger," who had the barge and equipment needed to dig up mud from the bottom of the river and turn it over to landowners for the repair of their dikes.

According to the National Park Service, "All the farmers along the river were notified when the muddigger would arrive, so he could complete repairs to everyone's banks at the same time. The farmers shared the cost as well as helped one another make repairs during emergencies. The dikes connected these people not only by land but also by the need to survive."

The Burcham sisters had good reason to maintain the dikes. If the dikes were to fail, their house would have been isolated on an island in the Maurice River. The National Park Service put it bluntly: "For the Burcham sisters, maintaining their dikes [was] essential for preserving the entire homestead."

By the time the sisters took over the farm, all the other farmers along the Maurice River, with the exception of one neighbor, had allowed their dikes to "fall into disrepair," according to the National Park Service. "The farm to the east of the Burchams existed until the middle of the 1950s when its owner allowed the dike to fail, fearing that the Burchams would do the same; he would have been unable to afford to maintain the dike independently. As a result, the sisters had to raise their access road three feet and extend their dike eastward to act as a barrier between their dry land and the renewed marshland. With the submergence of [the neighbor's property,] the Burchams became the only extant dike farm on the Maurice River."

An early Burcham farmhouse. *Courtesy of Steelman Photographics.*

Shortly after Hurricane Agnes blew in and out in 1972, the New Jersey Department of Environmental Protection notified the Burcham sisters and other property owners along the Maurice River that they could no longer use mud from the riverbed to build up or to repair their dikes. In response to the directive from the state, Janice and Jeanette had to look around for other materials they could use to keep their dike in good and reliable condition.

What they turned to and depended on was a combination of concrete (without reinforcement rods), crushed oyster and clamshells. Fortunately, oyster and clamshells are almost always available in South Jersey. In addition to finding a way to use materials other than mud to repair and maintain their dike, the sisters discovered that the same materials made a reliable path connecting their home and property to the mainland. This connection enabled future repairs to the dike to be made from the land; previously, of course, repairs had been made from the riverside.

In 2004, when the sisters were interviewed by Debra Barsotti, they pointed out that dike maintenance remained a major concern. According to Barsotti's report, the sisters guessed that "it would take only a few nor'easters or the wake of fast boats to wipe out all their work. It's costly to maintain the dike. The concrete, gravel and clam shells have been donated, but the laborers need to be paid." The sisters also laid to rest a few "misconceptions." For example, they said that they had never grown salt hay, although from earliest times on the river, the growing of salt hay had been commonplace. Again, unlike many farms in Cumberland County, they did not grow crops for sale. "The vegetables fed the family and the laborers."

According to Barsotti, "Janice and Jeanette…never expected to live out their lives on the family property. Their parents had aspirations for them and saw that they finished their four years at Millville High School and continued to college. Still, college was the first time the twin sisters were separated. They acknowledged the detrimental effect [going away to college] had on both of them during their first months apart. They both recalled how they lost weight and agreed that they both experienced a real sense of loss."

Of course, the sisters did live out their lives together on the Burcham farm, protected by the dike. As Barsotti put it at the end of her article about the remarkable Burchams and their farm protected by dike, "Decades slipped away. [The sisters'] worldly travels became another memory as the Burcham sisters occupied themselves with the daily upkeep of the family property. It was home—it is history. Future generations will be fortunate if preservation efforts can protect the legacy that the Burcham twins worked a lifetime to hold onto."

Chapter 12

HATS OFF TO THE "NEW" LANDIS THEATRE

I t was a week before the first day of spring, still cool in South Jersey, but the city of Vineland had planned a warm reception for the Landis Theatre, which opened its doors for the very first time that night of March 12 in the year 1937. The marquee announced that Mae Clark was starring in *Hats Off*, the new "enchanting musical romance."

The press release for that opening night noted that the theater had been constructed from plans drawn by William H. Lees, renowned architect of New York and Philadelphia, and that it had been built by a crew of seventy-five men who had begun working there since the previous November. It went on to say that the theater "represents the most advanced design in motion picture theatre buildings. Provision has been made for future innovations in film projection and sound, including television." The new theater, one of the largest and most beautiful in all of southern New Jersey at the time, had a seating capacity of 1,200. The news release boasted that the theater's "chairs," which were twelve inches wide, had "red-covered backs and leather covered seats." Aisles were thirty-two inches wide.

"As one enters the theatre," noted the news release, "it is seen that the lobby or outer foyer is a combination of blue and white arranged in circular design. Blue mirrors are framed in stainless steel, and the doors are of brown stained gumwood." At either end of the main foyer were "large louvres" that also served as air conditioning ducts. Flower boxes were placed at the bottom of the louvres. "The walls are paneled in grained gumwood, and the ceilings are painted in deep aquamarine. Lounges, modernly equipped, are

The Landis Theatre in Vineland as it looked in the mid-1900s.

at either end of the man foyer." The news release reported that restrooms were at either end of the foyer and that the ladies' restrooms included "powder rooms."

The theater was probably ahead of its time insofar as providing assistance for patrons who were deaf. "Western Electric 'Mirrorphonic' sound equipment has been installed in the big projection booth. An innovation here is a block of seats equipped with Western Electric earphones attached to the chairs for those who are hard of hearing."

The gala opening night ceremony featured singing of the national anthem, led by Training School superintendent C. Emerson Nash, and a "brief" welcoming address by Herbert Lubin, theater manager. Other speeches were delivered by Vineland mayor Samuel I. Gaasel; John H. Weed, chairman of the Landis Township Committee; and U.S. representative Elmer H. Wene.

In addition to the Landis Theatre being *the* place where residents of Cumberland County and beyond could view Hollywood's latest movies in comfort and splendor, it also was intended to be *the* place where audiences could view the best vaudeville acts touring the country.

Chapter 13

STILL NUMBER ONE

W hen it comes to the market value of nursery stock, Cumberland County ranks first in New Jersey and fifth in the United States. However, "the nursery business took a hit three or four years ago," according to James R. Johnson, county agricultural agent for nursery management, when the slowdown in the economy caused many developers to put off plans for building houses and commercial buildings. Consequently, there was a reduced demand for sod and nursery stock. However, Mr. Johnson pointed out that longtime and new homeowners have continued to purchase flowering plants and shrubs to enhance their properties.

Mr. Johnson, who has been Cumberland County agent for thirty years, has witnessed changes in the nursery industry. Three decades ago, he said, "The industry was very heavily into trees and shrubs—including such 'woodies' as yew, rhododendron, azalea and holly. They were the primary sales area at that time." Shortly thereafter, herbaceous perennials—plants that die down in the winter and come back in the spring—became very popular. According to Mr. Johnson, when he became agricultural agent three decades ago, "woodies" accounted for nearly 90 percent of the nursery business. Today, they make up 20 to 30 percent of industry sales. Interestingly, Mr. Johnson said, one of the reasons homeowners now prefer herbaceous perennials over the "woodies" is because they now prefer the color in their gardens that "woodies" cannot satisfy.

The reasons for the major shift also have to do with changes in the marketplace and the desire on the part of nursery owners to maintain income flow, said Mr. Johnson.

James Johnson, Cumberland County agricultural agent for nursery management. *Photo by Stephan A. Harrison.*

In the nursery business there are essentially two variables that determine whether you will make money or not. The first is the time that it takes for the product to mature to the point when it can be harvested. The second variable is how much space does it take to grow [the plant, shrub or tree]. *In other words, the nurseryman has a certain amount of land; if he can grow more plants on that certain piece of land, he can make more money, and if he can turn the crop over faster, he can make more money. For example, herbaceous perennials don't take as much space as a big shrub and don't take nearly as much time to grow; therefore, nurserymen may be forced into what to grow based on economic considerations.*

Today, Mr. Johnson said, people talk about certain trees or shrubs or plants as being invasive. They generally refer to those items that were brought to this part of the world from some other place. For example, he said, the common periwinkle was imported from Europe and planted by Europeans settling in this country. Another common invasive import is the red maple. "It grows all over the place," he said. "My only gripe when it comes to trying to control it is that at this point it has been around for two hundred years, and it's a little late now."

Some critics complain that homeowners waste water by putting too many sprinklers on too much lawn too often. On the other hand, Mr. Johnson pointed out that the nursery industry has been the driving force behind conducting water quality testing in recent years, especially here in Cumberland County. In the 1990s, he said, his office and others looked specifically at the upper Cohansey River watershed to determine the impact that agriculture and other activities were having on the river. The nursery industry wanted to know what impact, if any, it was having on the watershed and what it could do about it.

The industry also wanted to make sure that if there *was* a negative impact on the watershed, nurseries were not blamed if they were not responsible. One of the findings of the industry's work was that too much soil has washed into the river, creating silt. According to Mr. Johnson, about $700,000 has been earmarked for remediation of the problem.

Of course, he said, in the case of Cumberland County being the primary agricultural county in the state, there always will be environmental issues no matter what is done. "If we have major rainstorms shortly after farmers have just plowed before planting, there's not much you can do [to prevent some soil from washing away]. The soil's going to move. The only option is to remove agriculture from the area. Farmers now do just about as much as they can do, but there always will be issues."

What's the future for the nursery business in Cumberland County? It continues to serve homeowners and businesses along the East Coast, said Mr. Johnson. "And the climate here is just about right, one of the best from the Carolinas to New England."

Chapter 14

LONG AGO IN BRIDGETON

Early white settlers in the land that became Cumberland County had a problem that needed solving. Because the river (named for the Lenape Indian chief Cohansey) made it hard or impossible for people and their wagons to go from the western half of what was to become the new county split off from Salem to the eastern half, and vice versa, a bridge had to be built. And it was, sort of, and the place where the "bridge" was put down was called, naturally, Cohansey Bridge or Bridge-towne (neither name was all that official at the time). However, putting down a permanent bridge—an acceptable one, at least—was no simple matter, and eventually, the subject of bridge building and bridge placement became a contentious issue.

The first bridge, built before 1716 at a point where the river begins narrowing (around today's Hampton Street), was not very substantial and couldn't carry wagons. Plus, it was under water at high tide. In 1774, two years before America declared its independence, there was, according to the historians Cushing and Sheppard, "quite a strife concerning the bridge, Col. Enos Seeley desiring to have it placed at Broad Street, while Alexander Moore desired to have it rebuilt on the old site. It contained no draw at that time." While Seeley and Moore argued back and forth, John Moore White came along and offered to build a draw. He also had a plan for building wharves.

It wasn't until the summer of 1799, seven years after Cumberland became a county, that the board of freeholders became involved in the bridge issue. Cushing and Sheppard described what action the board of freeholders took:

South Jersey Institute in Bridgeton.

At the meeting of Aug 7, 1799, the board resolved to build a new bridge, "considerably wider than the present one," and at the next meeting, in September, they adopted a plan for a bridge with stone abutments and sixteen feet wide. The stone abutment on the east side was built that year. In December, the board resolved to make the bridge 21 feet and nine inches wide in the clear, and to support it on posts, and not on two piers in the river as was at first proposed...The whole cost of the bridge, exclusive of the draw, which was paid by Mr. White, was about $3,000.

Well, of course, that was not the end of bridge building, and the town earned its name over and over again. Early on, while the place had one or more names, it didn't have many inhabitants—hardly any, in fact. Before anyone thought about naming the place, Richard Hancock, who had had a falling-out with the intrepid but not so nice John Fenwick, acquired land when Cumberland was still Salem and built a sawmill on the river called Cohansey, or on one of its offshoots.

Sharon Morita, in her book about Bridgeton, wrote this about the mill's location: "The exact location of Hancock's sawmill is difficult to pinpoint because small offshoots of the Cohansey River have been dammed and undammed throughout the intervening years. Portions of land now above water

90

Bridgeton residence of Francis B. Minch.

were below the waterline in Hancock's day. The mill was perhaps built near the present junction of South Avenue and Grove Street. The mill processed the plentiful cedar timber much in demand for the building of Philadelphia." Indeed, at one point, some twenty-five sailing ships regularly transported up to twenty-five thousand cords of wood to Philadelphia on a regular basis.

Seventy or so years later, on the west side of the river, Silas Parvin built a two-storied house with a hip roof and a tavern. Parvin realized, of course, that travelers in the mid-1700s, before the Revolution, could stand a shot of whiskey if they were traveling long, hard roads.

In the year 1748, Cohansey Bridge or Bridge-towne looked pretty much like the following layout in comparison to subsequent development: Parvin's house and tavern was situated just south of present-day Commerce Street (there wasn't much north of that street) and east of Atlantic Street. The roads west toward Greenwich followed pretty much the same course as they do today: up the hill past where today's courthouse stands to Lawrence Street and then on toward Greenwich.

Jeremiah Sayre, a shoemaker (don't these names sound familiar even today?), lived in a house not far from today's courthouse, and on the site of the present courthouse was the house and shop belonging to the blacksmith John Hall. Hall's house was adjacent to the courthouse then

South Jersey Institute. *Courtesy of Lummis Research Library.*

existing. Hall also managed a tavern. One suspects that with the tavern next to the courthouse, Hall also had frequent customers whose business was attending to the law and those who violated it. Alas, unfortunately for weary travelers, lawyers and their clients and judges, Hall's house and tavern and the courthouse all burned to the ground in 1758.

One of the earliest and most extensive land purchases involved a man named Alexander Moore, who bought 990 acres that included much of the land located on the east side of the river that later became part of Bridgeton and running north to an area called Indian Fields. Cushing and Sheppard reported that

> *two years* [after the land purchase, Moore] *had a town laid out for him on the east side of the river by Daniel Elmer, Jr., a surveyor, which he called Cumberland. He sold a few lots by this plan, but only two of the streets were opened for a short distance, and that plan was never carried out. Moore was the first person who kept a store at Cohansey Bridge, as far as is known. He built a home on the north side of Commerce Street, which stood about sixty feet west of the present Cohansey Street, and his store-house, built of cedar logs, stood on the corner of present day Commerce and Cohansey Streets.*

With the issue pretty much settled as to where and how to build the bridge(s) needed to make Bridgeton the center of the county, the city went about becoming an industrial hub. Among the early plants were those making glass and woolen goods. Also, the city boasted several canneries. Cushing and Sheppard described them:

> *The Diamond Packing Company located on the river at the foot of Eagle Street has a capacity of one million cans annually. They employ 250 men, women and children during the season. The West Jersey Packing Company…is situated on Irving Avenue, about one-half mile from the built-up portion of the city, and puts up about the same number of cans and employs about the same number of hands. The canning factory of John W. Stout is…situated on the southeast corner of Bank Street and Irving Avenue, near the West Jersey Railroad depot. About 175 hands are employed here during the three or four months of the canning season, and they put up about 700,000 cans. The canning factory of Benjamin A. Ayars is on Water Street below Vine. He employs over 100 hands and puts up over 300,000 cans of goods.*

Bridgeton today boasts the largest historical district of any town in New Jersey, with more than two thousand properties on the national register. Richard Hancock, Colonel Seeley and Alexander Moore would be most pleased.

Chapter 15

LONG AGO IN
COMMERCIAL TOWNSHIP

Think about Commercial Township. What comes to mind? Oysters, right? Sure, the village of Port Norris was once the oyster capital of the world, but did you come up with sheep? Probably not. You won't find many sheep in the township today. But two centuries ago, you could count sheep in the thousands, and not in your sleep. It was thanks to "Coffee" Jones.

Two years before the War of 1812, Joseph "Coffee" Jones, the son of a rich coffee merchant in Philadelphia, arrived in that southern part of Cumberland County that would officially become Commercial Township in 1874. One might have expected him to invest time and money in buying up hundreds of acres of woods, and he did; one might also have expected him to see the potential for harvesting oysters from the Delaware Bay, but he didn't. Instead, he decided to raise sheep.

Of course, Jones started the business of raising sheep without knowing anything about the business of raising sheep. He engaged several men who knew more than he did to help him purchase sheep from farms throughout the counties of southern New Jersey, and he located and hired a Welshman by the name of David Owen to be shepherd in chief. With Owen's guidance, Jones located and purchased three Merino rams to help father his flock. He paid $900 for them, a *very* considerable sum in that day. Jones had built, also at considerable expense, a sheep pen that measured three hundred feet by sixty feet.

Then the rams started to prove that they were worth the exorbitant fee Jones paid to get them. Eventually, according to historians Thomas Cushing

A Port Norris office scene.

A Port Norris street scene. *Collection of the Bayshore Center at Bivalve.*

and Charles Sheppard, "There were literally thousands of sheep owned by Jones." It is doubtful that they all could be traced to those three rams. In any event, the sheep far outnumbered the human residents of the township at the time. "Many of the lambs were caught by foxes, which were then

A Port Norris school. *Courtesy of Lummis Research Library.*

numerous in that locality. The sheep appeared to fare well enough for awhile, but after the great northeast storm…in 1812…in which the large sheepfold was blown down, all of them died save about 300. It is said that the poor animals died faster than two [shearers] could take off their pelts." What wool Jones did get off his sheep sold, at the time, for one dollar per pound.

Eventually, as his herd became depleted, Jones lost interest in being king of the shepherds in southern New Jersey, and he sold the remaining sheep, about three hundred, to a party or parties on Hog Island up the Delaware River. "Thus ended the sheep speculation at Port Norris," reflected Cushing and Sheppard. "There are now few, if any, sheep in the neighborhood."

The village of Port Norris in the township was named for the son of notorious shepherd "Coffee" Jones. When Jones was not buying, selling or losing sheep, he was engaged in land speculation, and like he was when it came to sheep, he bought and sold land on a lavish scale. Again, Cushing and Sheppard related what happened: "Coffee Jones, disheartened and disgusted [about the sheep business] made a lottery of his real estate, selling the tickets wherever he could. It might be added that Jones' cleared and meadow land was divided into four-acre lots under 4,700 panel of fence, but a man gunning for a fox one day accidentally set fire to the meadow grass and almost totally burned the fence up."

The Samuel Shinn House (dating to circa 1877) in Port Norris. *Photo by Stephan A. Harrison.*

Ship captain's house in Port Norris, first occupied by Ichabod Compton Jr. in 1812. *Photo by Stephan A. Harrison.*

As if residents of the township hadn't seen more than enough sheep, decades later they had to endure more than too many rattlesnakes. According to a newspaper account of the day, one Ichabod Compton heard crows making a racket as they flew in and out of an island located

Egg Harbor Lighthouse. *Collection of the Bayshore Center at Bivalve.*

Walking the deck at Bivalve.

in a swamp next to his farm. It was early spring. "While in pursuit of the crows, he was startled by the sight of a large rattlesnake. He killed this and another of the same kind that afternoon, and returning the next day he killed seven more, the last of which he found coming out of a hole in the

The 1808 Thomas Lee House in Port Elizabeth. *Courtesy of Lummis Research Library.*

ground. This circumstance led to the suspicion that this might be the place where the whole battalion had their usual winter quarters." According to the newspaper account, Compton and his two brothers began digging in and around the hole in the ground and eventually unearthed twenty-eight rattlesnakes, "one large spotted snake, and four black snakes. All of these reptiles were in a torpid state."

The newspaper article went on to report that "several dens of similar description had been discovered in the neighborhood of Buckshutum, in all or most of which several kinds of snakes, and also frogs, were found grouped together." Cushing and Sheppard then reassured their readers that, while rattlesnakes "formerly abounded in the swamps along Maurice River, at the present day few, if any, of those reptiles can be found."

Of course, Commercial Township and the village of Port Norris have gained fame over the years—not for the sheep or the rattlesnakes and not even for the flamboyant "Coffee" Jones, but for their connection down the Maurice River to the Delaware Bay and oysters. In the nineteenth century, the families living in the township were already attached by a kind of umbilical cord to the bay and beyond. Shipbuilding had replaced raising sheep, and according to Cushing and Sheppard, "A large proportion of the

Dr. Willetts, a Civil War
officer of Port Elizabeth.
*Courtesy of Lummis
Research Library.*

male inhabitants [in the nineteenth century] lead a seafaring life, many of whom are captains of large coasting vessels, trading among the different ports from Maine to the West India Islands, and some of them to South American and European ports. These [seafaring men] have large and very convenient residences, and the town is one of the handsomest of the smaller places in the county."

However, Cushing and Sheppard added a kind of postscript to the success story. While seafaring men at the time made good money, and "while that business in general has been prosperous, and money has been acquired by many of them, their absence from home in the pursuit of their business has prevented that development of this portion of the county and its resources which would undoubtedly have taken place if these enterprising men had acquired their means from other sources."

Chapter 16

LONG AGO IN
DEERFIELD TOWNSHIP

I n the last decades of the nineteenth century, hundreds of thousands of Russian Jews immigrated to the United States to escape the persecution unleashed by the government then in power. A number of these refugees settled in southern New Jersey, and two of their primary colonies were located in Deerfield Township at Carmel and Rosenhayn.

Many of the Jewish families who came by ship from Russia to New York City boarded trains heading south into New Jersey. Although only a minority of the adults had been farmers in Russia, the trains took the families into two of the state's foremost and most prosperous agricultural centers: Cumberland and Salem Counties. Initially, in 1882, seventeen refugees got off the train in Carmel, but in less than two years, discouraged by the results of their few farming skills, seven of the original settlers left the area. However, other families followed, and by 1889, the colony at Carmel had grown to 286 persons.

According to the *Jewish Encyclopedia*, "82 of their children attended the public school. The farms comprised 864 acres, of which the Jewish colonists occupied 848 acres, although only 123 were under cultivation. Corn, rye, buckwheat, vegetables and berries were the chief crops. During the winter, the farmers supported themselves by tailoring."

According to the *Jewish Encyclopedia*, life was often hard for the families at Carmel. "The condition of the colony at Carmel [was] one of varying prosperity and depression. Outside aid, either by the establishment of local industries, by liberal loans on mortgages at a low rate of interest, or

Rosenhayn farmers' market, circa early 1900s. *Courtesy of Lummis Research Library.*

even by direct gifts, was, from time to time, necessary to enable the colony to exist."

Rosenhayn, which eventually became the larger of the two Jewish settlements in Deerfield Township, started off, at least in the mind of Joseph W. Morton, as a planned community, similar to what was designed for Vineland. Historians Thomas Cushing and Charles Sheppard, writing in the 1800s before the arrival of Jewish settlers from Russia, stated that shortly after the end of the Civil War, Morton made plans for making this part of the township a carbon copy of the residential layout in Vineland just across the township border. "Morton sold some of the lots, and a few houses were built, but he was not able to make [the area] a rival of Vineland, which had secured a few years' start, and after which Rosenhayn was planned." According to the historians, at the time of their writing (early in the 1880s), the settlement known as Rosenhayn contained fifteen to twenty houses and seventy-five inhabitants.

The Jewish settlers who arrived in Rosenhayn from New York City later in the 1800s were sponsored by the Hebrew Emigrant Aid Society. The *Jewish Encyclopedia* describes how they fared:

[In 1888, after a few Jewish families had settled in the area,] *37 additional families settled in the neighborhood, where they were sold farm land on the condition that they should build houses and cultivate a certain part of their holdings within a specified time. This agreement imposed hardships on the colonists, for, in order to meet their payments, they had to work at tailoring. For some time they lived and toiled in a large wooden building opposite the Rosenhayn railroad station. By the latter part of 1889, the Jewish settlers owned 1,912 acres at Rosenhayn, of which, however, only 261 acres were under cultivation—producing chiefly berries, corn and grapes. There were 67 families living in 23 houses, six of which were built by local Jewish carpenters. The population at that time amounted to 294.*

While the Jewish families grew in numbers in the township, the majority of original settlers were Presbyterian, the first families coming into the area in about 1730. The first church building, a simple log structure, was built in 1737 by members who had come to the area from New England. According to Cushing and Sheppard, "In the original humble temple men of great distinction at different times preached, such as Edwards, Blair, Gilbert, Tennant, and Finley, and it is very probable that George Whitefield did not pass Deerfield by, for it is known that he traveled through this region in the spring and fall of 1740 and preached at Pittsgrove, Greenwich and Salem."

Cushing and Sheppard cited a peculiar incident that occurred in the Deerfield Presbyterian Church in about 1765. Reverend Simon Williams, who had recently been named the church pastor and who stayed only two years,

on one occasion rode up to a certain house in his parish and, approaching the lady of he house, remarked, "Madame, I have selected your funeral text"; in reply to her inquiry, "What is it?," he answered, "You will find it in Acts Chapter 9, Verse 31: 'Then had the church rest.'" The Rev. R. Hamill Davis, in his very valuable and interesting history of the Deerfield Church, from which the principal facts in this sketch are obtained, observes, "The sin of which that woman was guilty has unsettled more pastors than all other causes combined."

Now, unless the historians listed the wrong Bible passage, it is difficult to determine how chapter 9, verse 31 of Acts would have chastened the woman and "unsettled" church pastors thereafter. The King James translation of the New Testament, which probably would have been the version read in the 1760s, quotes chapter 9, verse 31 of Acts as follows:

"Then had the churches rest throughout all Judea and Galilee and Samaria, and were edified; and walking in the fear of the Lord and in the comfort if the Holy Ghost, were multiplied."

Concerning the churches of that time in Deerfield and elsewhere in the area, Lucius Q.C. Elmer, in his book *History of the Early Settlement and Progress of Cumberland County*, pointed out that

very few churches in this region were warmed with fires until after the commencement of the present century [nineteenth], *and they were not then introduced without much opposition from old people who thought them needless, if not dangerous.*

For many years, a stove was not to be had, and open fireplaces, which were alone used in dwellings, were not suitable for a church. After stoves were introduced, so long as wood continued to be burned, that is to say until about twenty or twenty-five years since, they did not comfortably warm the buildings, it being common for females to have footstoves in their seats.

Chapter 17

LONG AGO IN
DOWNE TOWNSHIP

News flash to today's residents of Downe Township: your address should be Downes Township. However, don't change stationery, checks, driver's licenses or other important documents. The "s" was left off more than two hundred years ago and never reattached. Here is what happened.

When Cumberland parted company with Salem, the area now officially Downe Township was included as part of Fairfield Township. For whatever reason, Governor William Franklin, illegitimate son of Benjamin, decided to exercise a delegated (but never before used) power to create a new township from an existing one and give it a title. Governor Franklin, in his infinite wisdom, decided to name the new township to honor his wife, whose maiden name was Elizabeth Downes. Through a clerical error (sound familiar?), the "s" was dropped from the act incorporating the township in 1798.

Not only did the township lose an "s," it also lost land that became Commercial Township. However, Downe was originally part of Fairfield Township, so the deal could be called a land swap.

One could get the impression that Downe Township was cursed because of Governor Franklin's slight of hand. Thomas Cushing and Charles Sheppard, writing in the late 1800s, lamented that

> *with no manufactories within its limits, the greater portion of* [the township's] *soil a salt marsh, or so light as to be uninviting to the settler, with scant means of communication with places outside of its own limits, and with roads neglected and little attention paid to the thorough cultivation*

An aerial view of Fortescue in Downe Township. *Courtesy of Lummis Research Library.*

of the soil, as seems almost inevitably to be the result where nature bestows her gifts of food freely to those who have only to gather the crops, it is not to be wondered at that Downe Township has not increased as have some other portions of the county.

The historians reported that the township's population in 1870 was 1,687. By contrast, the population in 2000 was 1,631.

In those late decades of the nineteenth century, many of the male residents of the township worked in the thriving oyster industry and were away from home most days of the week. However, if many of the local men were away harvesting and processing oysters, there were enough of them at home to take care of the growing number of tourists, who had learned about the cool, fragrant breezes off the bay and found them in the township, and particularly at Fortescue.

At the time, men and women—couples mostly, perhaps some children— would come to Fortescue by boat or overland by stagecoach. Many would stay at the Country Tavern or the Fortescue Hotel, which advertised its "wharf and beach." The Country Tavern, perhaps more rustic than the hotel, was set back some three hundred feet from the bay and was shaded by trees that stood far above the tavern and the barns to the rear of the main house.

Fortescue was named for John Fortescue, who, in the same year that America declared its independence from Great Britain, sold to William Smith ten thousand acres in lower Downe Township. However, the summer resort named for Mr. Fortescue covered less than a dozen acres. While Cushing and Sheppard referred to Fortescue as "a place of summer resort, well known throughout all this region," they evidently believed that the appeal of the resort was fading. Writing in 1883, they labeled "the present buildings," which, presumably included the tavern and hotel, as "inconvenient and far from handsome, having been added to from time to time. A pier 1,125 feet long was built in 1880 [three years before the historians' major work] for a landing place for a steamboat which was then intended to be run to this place from Philadelphia, but that plan faded away, and the boats ceased running after a few weeks."

The *Historical Collections of the State of New Jersey*, dated 1844, offers a description of the village of Dividing Creek, but it is missing a tagline that should read, "Guess Who?" Here is the description: "Dividing Creek is near the central part of the township, on a creek of the same name, and 16 miles from Bridgeton. It has a Methodist and a Baptist church and about 40 dwellings. One of the present members of the United States Senate from Mississippi was bred a shoemaker in this village, and by his enterprise and industry won the way to his present station. Charles Brown, now a member of Congress from Pennsylvania, was also bred here." Now, guess who was the senator from Mississippi who grew up in Dividing Creek?

If that description had been written, say, twenty years later, the reader might understand why the name of a senator from the Confederate States of America might have been omitted, but not in 1844. After conducting a search of existing records, I am pleased to report that the unnamed senator from Mississippi who grew up in Dividing Creek is none other than John Henderson, who was born in Cumberland County, presumably in or near Dividing Creek, on February 28, 1797. The family moved south to Mississippi some years later. He served one term in the U.S. Senate, from 1839 to 1845.

The *Historical Collections* quoted above makes mention of the Dividing Creek Baptist Church. Cushing and Sheppard also wrote about the same church…for almost two pages. Apparently, in the middle of the nineteenth century, there was quite a turnover in church pastors, perhaps due to the fact that, again according to Cushing and Sheppard, "in March, 1855, the church dismissed 51 members to constitute the Newport Baptist Church."

Concerning the rapid turnover in pastors before and after the "dismissal," the historians had this to say:

The Rev. Henry W. Weber succeeded [Reverend George Sleeper] in [1859], and remained two years. In the autumn of 1861, the Rev. Alexander H. Folwell succeeded him and resigned in February, 1863. The Rev. Benjamin Jones became pastor in August 1863 and, after a connection of less than two years, resigned. In 1865, the Rev. E. V. King became pastor, but did not continue more than one year. He returned to the Methodists. The Rev. Lathrop W. Wheeler was pastor from 1866 to 1868. In 1869, the Rev. James H. Hyatt became pastor and remained a little over a year.

Cushing and Sheppard made a point of stating that after the rapid turnover of pastors and the "dismissal" of 51 members in the middle years of the nineteenth century, the Dividing Creek Baptist Church still had a healthy congregation of 176 in the 1880s.

Chapter 18

LONG AGO IN
FAIRFIELD TOWNSHIP

Fairfield, Connecticut, is just down the coast from Bridgeport, and Fairfield Township in Cumberland County is just down the coast from Greenwich. Of course, it is also right next door, so to speak, to Bridgeton.

Toward the end of the seventeenth century, an indeterminate number of families left their homes in Connecticut and traveled south until they settled in the vicinity of what is still referred to today on Cumberland County maps as New England Crossroads in Fairfield Township. Of course, winter may be easier to get through in southern New Jersey than in Connecticut, and land once inhabited by Lenape Indians along the Cohansey River was still unspoiled and there for the taking (or settling), but it is not known for certain why those families and a few families from Long Island moved south.

In any event, they came, and according to historians Thomas Cushing and Charles Sheppard, "Their enterprise and thrift made them prosperous." What contributed primarily to their early prosperity, according to the historians, was the rich "sandy loam" they found in the area. The soil was "well suited to the raising of fruits and [vegetables,] large quantities of which are annually raised. The eastern portion of the township is mostly covered with oak and pine in various stages of growth."

Of course, newcomers from up north, like the Indians before them, tended to settle on or near the Cohansey River and its tributaries. The Cohansey River not only supplied water for irrigating crops and feeding livestock, but the waterway was also the route for ships carrying cargo out to

Bicyclers at Clark's Pond in Fairton, circa 1894. *Courtesy of Lummis Research Library.*

Philadelphia and elsewhere, as well as for ships bringing goods from the city and elsewhere to the settlers.

Two of the early industries on the bank of the river were a sawmill and gristmill built by Samuel Fithian and at least seven other men whose names as co-owners were never listed. They all had come to the area from Connecticut on or about 1700.

A mystery of sorts surrounds the mills. Cushing and Sheppard reported that during the American Revolution, vague reference was made to an ironworks there. "Diligent inquiry has failed to give any more light as to the character of these iron works, but there was probably a furnace for the smelting of the bog iron ore, deposits of which were found in the swamps of Downe and probably of Fairfield also," they wrote. "During the [American] Revolution, the furnace at Batsto in the interior of the pine region, beyond the incursions of the British, was engaged in the casting of cannon and other materials of war for the supply of the American army, and it may be that this furnace [belonging to Mr. Fithian] was used for a like patriotic purpose."

The Fithian sons carried on the business well into the nineteenth century. In 1801, Amos Fithian, a descendant of Samuel, was referred to as one of the leading citizens of Fairfield, and the mills begun by his ancestor were doing a brisk business.

Some early settlers in the area called their small neighborhood Kill-pig-hole. The name is thought to have originated when a pig wandered into a pit filled with quicksand. In any event, residents of the area finally grew tired of trying to explain to later arrivals how their neighborhood got its name—if, in fact, they actually knew—and so the area was renamed Rockville.

Speaking of name changes, Fairton, today the principal community in the township, was once called Bumbridge. Cushing and Sheppard explained how the town originally got what today would be considered an unflattering title. The name "was said to have originated from the circumstances of a constable, who was then often called a bum-bailiff, [which was] a corruption of bound bailiff, or a bailiff bound with security, having fallen through the bridge over Rattlesnake Run while attempting to arrest a person. This caused the bridge to be repaired [and given a new name]. The name of Fairton was not given it until the post office was established [not until 1806]."

By any other name, in the 1800s Fairton was the site of a very successful slaughterhouse begun by Furman R. Willis and James McNichols with an investment of fifty dollars. Cushing and Sheppard explained what happened: "They first did an ordinary butchering business, selling their meats from house to house in the surrounding towns and country, but the same fall [of 1870, they] began putting up mince-meat for market. The first batch was a 38-pound bucket, but this branch of the business increased until they sold seven tons in one week. A large business is now [circa 1883] done in packing beef and pork, amounting to $60,000 a year and employing 13 hands."

Enterprising businessmen also prospered at a point where the extensive marshes that cover much of the township stop at the Delaware Bay. The place is called Sea Breeze. The businessmen, whose names have become lost in old records, bought one hundred or more acres along the bay in the 1870s and built an amusement pavilion featuring a merry-go-round and a steamboat landing that could attract pleasure boats coming down from Philadelphia. The men located a Civil War ordnance ship and turned it into an excursion vessel plying between Sea Breeze and points north. The same businessmen/speculators also built a forty-room hotel that, naturally, boasted a well-designed and well-stocked bar. Unfortunately, the hotel burned to the ground before the turn of the century.

One of the most historic and legendary areas of Fairfield Township is Gouldtown, located now on the main highway between Bridgeton and Millville. The legend begins, as do most pertaining to Salem and Cumberland Counties, with the land speculator John Fenwick and his family and followers in the seventeenth century. Samuel Johnson, in his *History of Fenwick's Colony*, wrote, "Among the numerous troubles and vexations which assailed Fenwick, none appear to have distressed him more than the base and abandoned conduct of his granddaughter, Elizabeth Adams, who had attached herself to a citizen of color." Fenwick, the Quaker, called the marriage between Elizabeth and the "citizen of color" an "abominable transgression." He never reconciled himself to the marriage and disinherited Elizabeth in his will. The black coachman whom Elizabeth wed was named Gould.

According to another history of Gouldtown, the area "has been dominated through the years alternately by Goulds and Pierces. Intermarriage with Indians and whites was common, even before the Revolutionary War. For generations, the two main branches of the community [Goulds and Pierces] followed separate paths of development. The Goulds were stolid conservatives, and, for nearly a century teetotalers, while the Pierces were long noted for their gaiety, love of music, dancing and generous drinking."

According to historical records, three out of four male residents of Gouldtown joined the American army in the Revolution. At the start of the Civil War, "The community officially notified President Lincoln that it could raise a regiment of colored men 'burning with a great zeal' to help defeat the armies of the slaveholders.' When that offer was rejected by the government, the entire community felt rebuffed. Scores of Gouldtown men quietly slipped away from their homes and joined the Union Army as white men."

Chapter 19

LONG AGO IN GREENWICH TOWNSHIP

J ohn Fenwick was not without faults—lots of them, in fact—but he knew and coveted good land when he found it. In the seventeenth century, he acquired (some would say appropriated) good land from the Lenape Indians that bordered the Delaware River and ran along the northern bank of the Cohansey River (also called the Ceasaria). That good land became Greenwich.

Shortly after he and his family members and landholders-to-be landed in what was still Salem County, the area that became Greenwich Township was divided into separate land parcels of sixteen acres each and made available to those families who had come with Fenwick. Although the settlement was called Greenwich, it also went by the Lenape Indian name Cohansey, which name also had been given to the river that brought the settlers in from the Delaware Bay.

One of the sixteen-acre lots was sold to Mark Reeve in August 1686. According to the *West Jersey History Project* in 2012, the lot was on the river, and Reeve built a house there:

> *In December of the same year, Reeve, in consideration of* [eighty pounds] *conveyed it to Joseph Browne, late of Philadelphia, "reserving to himself and his heirs a free egress and regress to and from a certain piece of ground, containing 24 square feet, where the said Mark Reeve's wife lies buried." Browne conveyed* [the land] *to Chalkey, a Friend, in 1738, and he to John Butler. Butler conveyed to Thomas Mulford, and he to William*

The Philip Sheppard House in Greenwich.

Conover, who conveyed it to John Sheppard, December 16, 1760, in whose family it has remained ever since.

Life in Greenwich in the early decades of the eighteenth century, especially for married women with families, is described in part by the following "interesting account of the Maskell Ewing family," provided by Lucius Q.C. Elmer in his book *Elmer's History of Cumberland County, New Jersey*:

His [Maskell's] wife was a woman of plain manners, though lady-like and very sensible. She was remarkable for her powers as a housekeeper. With the exception of her husband's Sunday coat, which was the one that had served at his wedding, and which lasted for a good part of [his] life, she had on hand the making of his and their children's garments from the flax and wool. All the bedding and house linen must be made and geese kept to find materials for beds; some thousand weight of cheese to be prepared annually for market; poultry and calves to be raised; gardening to be done; the work of butchering time to be attended to (this included the putting up of pork and salt meat to last the whole year, besides sausages for winter and the making of candles); herbs to be gathered and dried and ointments compounded; besides all the ordinary housework of washing,

115

Orthodox Friends Meetinghouse in Greenwich. *Courtesy of Lummis Research Library.*

ironing, patching, darning, knitting, scrubbing, baking, cooking and many other avocations which a farmer's wife nowadays would be apt to think entirely out of her line.

And all this without any "help," other than that afforded by her daughters as they became able; and for the first 22 years with a baby always to be nursed. This afforded no time for any reading but the best, but many a good book she contrived to read by laying it in her lap whist her hands plied the knitting needles, or to hear read by her husband or one of the children while she and the rest spent the evening in sewing. On the Sabbath, a folio Flavel, the Institute of Calvin and, above all, the Bible were the treasures in which her soul delighted.

According to the West Jersey History Project, a memorial dated 1701

prays that…the ports of Burlington and Cohansey [Greenwich] in West Jersey may be established ports of those respective provinces forever. An Act of the Assembly of West Jersey, in 1695, recites that a considerable number of people are settled in or about Cohansey…and enacts that there shall be two fairs kept yearly at the town of Greenwich at Cohansey aforesaid; the

An old tea house in Greenwich. *Courtesy of Lummis Research Library.*

Houses lining Ye Greate Street in Greenwich. *Courtesy of Lummis Research Library.*

first on the 24th and 25th days of April, and the second on the 16th and 17th
days of October. These fairs were continued and were largely attended until
1765, when a law was enacted reciting that fairs in the town of Greenwich
had been found inconvenient and unnecessary.

Supposedly, by 1765, local merchants had established themselves in the
bustling Greenwich, by then a major Delaware River port, and they believed
that the fairs, which attracted and sold merchandise to large crowds, had
become unfair competition. According to the National Park Service's book
Southern New Jersey and the Delaware Bay, another reason for closing down the
fairs was that "despite efforts to keep the fairs orderly, some outsiders caused
problems by selling liquor and encouraging horse racing. Some attempts
were made by local governments to curtail the unruliness. Nevertheless,
eventually the concept of fairs coinciding with market days was lost in an
atmosphere of gambling and drinking."

The local merchants were probably correct in their observations. In any
event, they prospered after the fairs departed. In his book, Elmer wrote that

Greenwich was the place of most business up to the beginning of the present
century [nineteenth]. *The stores there contained the largest assortment of*

goods. A young lady who visited Bridgeton in 1786 mentions, in a journal which has been preserved, going to Greenwich "to get her broken watch crystal replaced, but the man had not received any from Philadelphia as he expected." She mentions going to Wood and Sheppard's store to get a few trifles. They transacted so large a business as to make it worth while to have bonds printed payable to them.

The business in Greenwich in the last decades of the eighteenth century was enhanced, perhaps, when a ferry was established in 1768 to connect Greenwich with Fairfield Township to the south. The ferry service was owned and operated by John Sheppard, of Wood & Sheppard, who already owned the wharf property in Greenwich where the ferry would dock. The governing bodies of Greenwich and Fairfield agreed to lease the ferry rights to Sheppard for 999 years. In return, he agreed to maintain the ferryboat and the roads leading up to the wharves.

According to the West Jersey History Project, "About 1810, and again in 1820, efforts were made to have a drawbridge built at the expense of the county, but this project was strenuously resisted by those living on the river above and, [the project proposal] being defeated, caused much rejoicing. For several years a horse-boat was in constant use, but as other towns grew and

The Gibbon House, circa 1730, in Greenwich. *Courtesy of Lummis Research Library.*

capital increased, Greenwich lost its relative importance and the ferry had but little business." Therefore, in 1838, the governing bodies of Greenwich and Fairfield released John Sheppard, who was the son of the John Sheppard who had made the agreement, from any further obligation in return for his paying the counties $300.

As previously mentioned, Greenwich was the center of business in Cumberland County from the time the county split from Salem in 1748 until almost the end of the century. However, Greenwich merchants and their customers had to cast an increasingly worried and jealous eye toward Bridgeton. Residents and merchants in Greenwich were shocked and not a little bit angry when, in 1748, while Greenwich was still bustling, the Cumberland County freeholders designated Bridgeton—while it was still called Bridge-towne—as the county seat.

Chapter 20

LONG AGO IN HOPEWELL TOWNSHIP AND SHILOH BOROUGH

In ancient times, three hundred years before the walled city of Jerusalem gained prominence, Shiloh was the religious capital of Israel. Some three hundred years ago in this country, the town of Shiloh, then called Cohansey Corners, gained prominence as a center for religious freedom.

Nowadays, those people who proclaim the seventh day of the week—Saturday—to be their Sabbath may be referred to as Seventh-day Baptists or Seventh-day Adventists. In 1687, when the Lenape Indians still practiced their sacred rituals in the land bordering the Cohansey River, Reverend Timothy Brooks brought down from Swansea, Massachusetts, to the area now known as Shiloh a small number of families who observed Saturday as their Sabbath. Some forty years later, when Robert Ayers came to Shiloh from Rhode Island along with a sizable number of other like-minded men and women, they were called Sabbatarians. The Sabbatarians, like the families from Swansea, based their faith on these three principles:

- God proclaimed the seventh day of the week as the Sabbath.
- God's proclamation is binding on mankind for all time.
- Nowhere in scripture is the first day of the week proclaimed to be the Sabbath.

Why these families from New England and later from other states, who were escaping religious persecution at home, chose the land along the west bank of the Cohansey River as their refuge is not entirely clear. What is

Whitaker dry goods and grocery in Roadstown. *Courtesy of Lummis Research Library.*

certain, however, is that Shiloh, which now exists as part inside Hopewell Township and part inside Stow Creek Township, became a shelter where they could practice their faith without hindrance.

Wrote Thomas Cushing and Charles Sheppard in 1883:

> *The history of the village* [of Shiloh] *is the history of the church,* [with] *very few, except the adherents of this faith* [Seventh-day Baptists] *residing within its limits. The surrounding country for a distance of from one to one and a half miles in all directions is filled with highly-cultivated farms, nearly all belonging to those of this faith. To one unaccustomed to the sight it seems out of place to find the people at work on their farms and in their shops and houses on the first day of the week, but if such a person will look in upon this community on the seventh day, and observe the scrupulous regard they show for the Sabbath as they view it, he must feel that only a conscientious conviction of the truth of their belief can inspire them in upholding the banner of Sabbatarianism, in the midst of surroundings which ever tend to change their adherents, especially the younger portion of them, to advocates of the keeping of the first day as the Sabbath.*

Long Ago in Hopewell Township and Shiloh Borough

Looking down West Avenue in Shiloh. *Courtesy of Lummis Research Library.*

A vigilant and vociferous defender of religious freedom, Reverend Nathaniel Jenkins became pastor of the church in Shiloh in 1730. Before coming to Shiloh, Mr. Jenkins had made a host of friends and a number of enemies as a member of the New Jersey State Assembly from Cape May. When he was in the state assembly, a fellow legislator introduced a bill that would "punish such persons as denied the doctrine of Trinity, the divinity of Christ, and the inspiration of the Scriptures." According to Cushing and Sheppard, "Mr. Jenkins stood boldly forth [in the state assembly] as the champion of soul liberty, declaring that, although he believed those doctrines as firmly as the warmest advocate of the ill-designed bill, he would never consent to oppose those who rejected them with law or with any other weapon than argument. As a result, the bill was quashed, to the great disappointment of those who would have the scenes of persecution which raged in New England repeated in New Jersey. The church grew under Mr. Jenkins' labors."

Various historical sources claim that the Sabbatarians, or Seventh-day Adventists, who settled Hopewell Township were "an intelligent people." Perhaps they earned that honorarium because of their commitment to education. The township, particularly the Shiloh area, was noted for its schools.

In 1848, the church-connected Union Academy was opened, with Professor E. Larkin in charge. Two years later, the Union Academy moved into the so-called Old Church in Shiloh, which had been remodeled for the school. In 1866, Union Academy again moved, this time into a brand-new two-story school building constructed of brick that had been erected for the then-substantial cost of $10,000. The first floor of the new building was used for recitation rooms and a laboratory, and the second floor was set aside for assemblies and other functions when all students and teachers were gathered together.

According to a history of the township written by a Rowan College student in 1997, although private sources had spent $10,000 on the Union Academy in 1848, public funds amounting to less than $5,000 paid for—count them—eight schoolhouses in 1896.

"There were 441 students enrolled and ten teachers employed," according to the student's report, which continued:

> Of the eight original schoolhouses, seven were heated by stoves, and it is not mentioned if they were wood or coal burning stoves. The Shiloh School was to have been heated by hot air and ventilated by gravity. The other seven schoolhouses were ventilated by windows. All these schools had outhouses but no electric. All were constructed of wood, except for the Shiloh School, which was constructed of brick. Five years later, in 1902, the Township allocated all of $5,091 for "educational expenses." The number of students enrolled in Township schools in that year was 485. A male teacher earned $40.70 per month and a female teacher earned $36.27.

Bowentown is still a dot on the map of Hopewell Township—a neighborhood, a crossroads. The area has been called Bowentown ever since Samuel Bowen arrived from Wales by way of Massachusetts toward the end of the seventeenth century. Like many of the original settlers of Hopewell Township, the Bowens were Baptists who had not been welcomed by Puritans in New England.

According to Cushing and Sheppard, the Bowen family not only fit into life in Cumberland County but also helped shape life there. David Bowen was appointed sheriff of Cumberland County on the eve of the American Revolution. Another Bowen, Jonathan Jr., represented the area at the 1776 convention that adopted New Jersey's first state constitution in 1776; he also was a member of the first state assembly. Jonathan served in the state assembly for seven terms, finally giving up his seat in 1800.

Chapter 21

LONG AGO IN LAWRENCE TOWNSHIP

L awrence Township was incorporated in 1885, but Cedarville, situated nearly in the center of the township, has been the township's heartbeat since before the American Revolution. Indeed, Lawrence family members, for whom the township presumably was named, were buying land and doing a brisk business in the early 1700s. Historical records show that Jonathan Lawrence got together with Amos Fithian, who may have been one of the "tea burners" in Greenwich, and engaged in a "considerable mercantile business." Norton O. Lawrence was exceedingly busy operating a country store on the one hand and, on the other, shipping lumber down Cedar Creek bound for Philadelphia. Norton Lawrence, who died in 1744, was a major landowner in the area. One historical account about Cedarville points out that "it is safe to assume that these types of businesses could only have been carried on where there were people to buy, so there were settlers, farmers and skilled laborers in the area at the time [pre-Revolution]."

Apparently, there were more than enough "skilled laborers" because an iron furnace, a gristmill, a sawmill and a shipbuilding yard were operating before and immediately after the Revolution. According to one account, the iron furnace was the first manufacturing business. It used local bog iron, and the forge house used for smelting the iron was forty feet long and thirty feet wide. There was one furnace. While no documents apparently exist that prove one way or another if the ironworks at Cedarville produced armaments during the Revolution, it is possible that it did.

Moving forward thirty or more years, historical records show how the fates and a typically sluggish federal bureaucracy operated even centuries ago. Take the case of Moses Burt of Lawrence Township. Burt was a loyal soldier in the New Jersey militia when it was called up for federal service at the start of the War of 1812. Because of his long and valued service in the militia, his name was submitted to state authorities and then on to the United States Congress for promotion to major in the federal army. Guess when Congress got around to granting his commission? April 1815. The war had ended thirty days earlier, on February 17.

At the conclusion of the Revolution, shipbuilding (which had almost ceased during the war) resumed, and it had become a major industry by the end of the nineteenth century. Most of the boats built were schooners and sloops. One schooner, named *Edna A. Pogue*, had three masts and weighed 162 tons. According to newspapers of the time, the Claypool and Parsons Shipyard had three boats under construction at the same time. The newspapers also recorded that the schooner *George W. McCowan* was constructed on property owned by the Corson family on Lummistown Road at the corner of North Avenue. After construction of the ship was completed, it was moved to water on specially built wheels.

Cedarville, which had been producing sloops and schooners for a number of customers and purposes, started building oyster boats at about the time that harvesting oysters became a major industry in the county, about 1870. At one time, nearly fifty oyster boats were berthed on Cedar Creek at Cedarville. According to one historical account, the Cedarville Landing was bustling for all of the last half of the nineteenth century and into the twentieth. "It was quite a sight to see: dozens of sailing ships, schooners, sloops and bugeyes at dock, at the Iron Bridge, and at the different reaches in the creek." The same account reported that "many skeletons of the old ships [lie] scattered along the banks of Cedar Creek, where the mud and marsh grasses have covered them."

One of the "big events" of the early nineteenth century was the opening of a Sabbath or Sunday school on the south side of the Cedar Creek dam. According to records, the school enrolled 191 students. "The first officers were the Rev. John Burt and Norton Lawrence. It was organized under the supervision of twelve men, one [of whom] was the Rev. Ethan Osborn." A church congregation also was formed at Cedarvillle in 1838. "Thirty-five [people] came with certificates from the Old Stone Church and from other churches. A new brick house of worship was started in 1839 and completed in 1840. It was thirty feet by fifty feet in size and was situated on the north side of the dam."

As the nineteenth century was coming to an end, Cedarville, at the heart of the newly formed Lawrence Township, was still a hub of activity. From the beginning, residents had found employment in the several industries in Cedarville, beginning in the middle of the eighteenth century. Then, in the last decades of the nineteenth century, the South Jersey Packing Company opened. At its busiest time, the company employed a large number of township residents, who turned out as many as 250,000 cans of vegetables.

Chapter 22

LONG AGO IN MAURICE
RIVER TOWNSHIP

This township, tucked into the southeast corner of the county, might have been called Wahatquenak if the Lenape Indians had had their way, which, of course, they didn't. Wahatquenak is the name the tribe gave to the Maurice River. White settlers named the river and the township after Prince Maurice, whose courtly name was lettered on the side of a ship allegedly burned by Indians in the river.

Not only did a foreign prince unknowingly lend his name to the township, but Elizabeth Clark Bodely also lent her first name to the principal village within the township: Port Elizabeth. Who was this Elizabeth who had an important inland port named for her?

Bodely was born in Pilesgrove Township in Salem County in 1737, when the area that later became Cumberland County was still a part of Salem County. She married the fairly moneyed Cornelius Clark of Burlington, and in the year 1757, about the time she celebrated her twentieth birthday, the newly married couple moved to the wilderness where the Manumuskin flowed into the Wahatquenak. They bought land along the Manumuskin Creek—some historians say it was thousands of acres—and built a log cabin that was considerably larger, of better construction and no doubt better furnished than most in the area.

Elizabeth was described as a woman of medium height, with dark eyes and a ready smile. According to one description:

She possessed an expanded mind and great benevolence of character. The poor in the neighborhood [of the Clark estate] *always found her to*

William J. Bradley was the largest schooner built on the Maurice River.

be a friend indeed. It is said there were very few days in the autumn and winter seasons when the poor were not found at her door receiving supplies of food and clothing. It frequently occurred, when the poor came to ask for assistance, that they would tell her some marvelous tales about witches, etc., to all of which she would listen without endeavoring to convince them to the contrary.

The newlyweds, however, were not the first white people to find their way to the riverbanks. For example, a small number of Swedish families had migrated to the area in the early 1700s and built their log homes on the same riverbanks. In 1743, the Swedes built a church. Incidentally, a man named John Bell had acquired a license for a tavern three years earlier.

The Clarks had four children: Joel, John, Susan and Elizabeth. Unfortunately, Cornelius, Elizabeth's husband, died not long after the birth of the children while still a young man. Elizabeth, left a widow with four children, continued to manage the family estate. It has been said that the land that Elizabeth managed after the death of her husband proved to be among the best meadowland in all of what became Cumberland County. Elizabeth later married John Bodely and had two children by him. She died in 1815 at the age of seventy-eight.

Looking up Buckshutem Road in Mauricetown.

Bricksboro in Maurice River Township. *Courtesy of Lummis Research Library.*

Property of Samuel Hilliard in Mauricetown. *Courtesy of Lummis Research Library.*

The town named for Elizabeth, Port Elizabeth, is located on the Manumuskin Creek where it joins the Maurice River. Elizabeth is credited with laying out the town pretty much as it exists now. Today, descendants of Lenape Indians who once lived along the banks of the Manumuskin Creek and the Maurice River, not far from early white settlers, have unsuccessfully (so far) laid claim to much of the land between Port Elizabeth and the Delaware Bay.

While the ancestors of today's generation of Lenape Indians were still living and fishing along the two waterways, ships left Port Elizabeth on a regular basis bound for the West Indies. Later, as noted in the chapter about glassmaking in Cumberland County, the enterprising James Lee came to the area and established a plant in Port Elizabeth that made window glass.

In 1778, the United States of America was only two years old, and Methodism had been exported from Great Britain to our shores not more than a dozen or so years earlier. One of the first "ordained" Methodist preachers was a reformed drunkard by the name of Benjamin Abbott. He had been "saved" by a Methodist circuit rider at a ceremony in a private home in Pittsgrove Township in Salem County. According to the historians Cushing and Sheppard, Abbott was "doubtless, the most remarkable man of early Methodism. [Abbott's] early life had been riotously wicked and,

A military tug docked at Dorchester Shipyard in 1945.

not withstanding the spirit of God [that] had often alarmed his guilty soul of its danger, he continued in sin until the fortieth year of age. In 1778, Abbott attended a quarterly meeting at Maurice River, very probably at Port Elizabeth. Doubtless about this time, a [Methodist] society was organized at [Port Elizabeth.]"

Abbott was, by all accounts, the most inflammatory of all the early "fire and brimstone" preachers. Reports exist that recall how his preaching cast a spell and often caused listeners to fall to the floor. The record does not report whether Elizabeth Clark Bodely attended one of Abbott's sessions and whether she may have declared herself to be a Methodist. But in any event, according to the historians,

> [On] *October 1, 1785,* [seven years after Abbott was said to have preached in Port Elizabeth,] *for the nominal sum of five shillings, Mrs. Elizabeth Bodely, who owned nearly all the land in the neighborhood of Port Elizabeth…gave a lot containing one acre and twenty-seven-hundreths, "for the purpose of building a preaching-house on and a burying-yard, and to build a schoolhouse for the use of the neighborhood after the said meeting-house is built."*

The Port Elizabeth Methodist Church, one of the first in New Jersey, was probably erected the following year in 1786.

Down the Maurice River about three and a half miles south of Port Elizabeth is the village of Dorchester. Just before the eighteenth century turned into the nineteenth, Peter Reeve purchased the land that became the village of Dorchester. At the time of his purchase, the community had only three houses, perhaps owned and lived in by ancestors of the Swedes who first immigrated to this part of Cumberland County. By the end of the nineteenth century, a century later, the population had grown to only 329. While the population of Dorchester did not grow substantially over the years, the village made its mark in Cumberland County because its male residents spent most of their time building sailing ships, a number of which went back and forth between Port Elizabeth and the West Indies.

Today, Leesburg in the township is the site of a state prison, but in 1795, the Lee brothers, both of whom were ship carpenters, came to settle in the area and had their family name attached to the settlement. Naturally, the brothers started building sailing ships that, like those leaving Port Elizabeth, first went to the West Indies and back. Later, ships built by the Lee brothers and other men sailed to Philadelphia and New York.

A much later arrival, in 1850, was James Ward. He built a marine railway that facilitated the repair of sailing ships and lasted for decades. Ward also was postmaster of Leesburg until his death in 1863.

Cushing and Sheppard, writing in the latter half of the nineteenth century, ended the opening section of their chapter on the township of Maurice River by stating that the township "increased rapidly in population in the latter part of the [eighteenth] and the beginning of [the nineteenth] century, but afterward lost its importance in the county, other portions increasing in population and business in a greater ratio." Today's residents of the township might, and *should*, take exception.

Chapter 23

LONG AGO IN MILLVILLE

Today's Millville owes a debt to yesterday's Joseph Buck. He pretty much invented the city in the decade after the American Revolution. In most references, Buck is referred to as Colonel Buck, but a self-described official New Jersey biography reports that he departed the army after the Revolution with the rank of captain. Perhaps he assumed the rank of colonel when he served as Cumberland County sheriff from 1787 to 1790. Whatever his rank, Buck was pretty much in command of the early development of Millville as a great place to live and as an industrial hub. To begin with, he, along with a few associates, bought up much of the woodland on either side of the Maurice River that today are the west and east banks of the river in the heart of the city. They also purchased land that included what is today Union Lake (then referred to as Union Pond), which feeds the Maurice River.

Colonel Buck's plan was to situate mills (hence why he named the settlement Millville) where Union Pond connected to the river. The mills, of course, would draw needed water from Union Pond. Also according to plan, houses would be built on either side of the Maurice River below the pond. By 1802, the year before Buck's death, only some of his plans had come to fruition. According to the historians Thomas Cushing and Charles Sheppard, "Colonel Buck and his associates did not carry out their plans of bringing the water down to the town, but mills were built at the pond. They sold a few lots in the town, on which houses were built. In 1802 [the year Buck died] the only houses were the ones on the west side of the river."

A house from the past in downtown Millville. *Photo by Stephan A. Harrison.*

Deliverance Hall in Millville, circa 1918. *Courtesy of Steelman Photographics.*

Crossing Fifth Street in Millville. *Courtesy of Steelman Photographics.*

Of course, by Independence Day in the year 1882, Millville was a bustling town. The holiday crowd on that July 4 in Millville attended the laying of the cornerstone for a building on High Street that would be home to a promising innovation called the Workingman's Institute.

The Workingman's Institute, with the backing of and bankroll from the glass industry giant Whitall Tatum Company, actually had opened the previous March in smaller, temporary quarters. Cushing and Sheppard described the purpose of the Workingman's Institute: "The Institute was organized in March, 1882. It comprised over 400 members and opened in a hall hired for the purpose, in which it provided games, music, lectures, debates, etc. and smoking and conversation was unrestrained. Three months of trial proved its success in attracting young men from the saloons. The absence of any rules of order placed them on their sense of propriety, and no case of rowdyism was had." The majority of men were employees in the glass industry, especially in the plants owned and operated by the Whitall Tatum Company.

In February 1883, less than a year after the cornerstone ceremony, the permanent home of the Workingman's Institute opened on High Street. "The opening was celebrated by a tea party given by the ladies of the city," reported Cushing and Sheppard. "The purpose of the Institute is to advance the moral

Above: Looking south from High and Pine Streets in Millville. *Courtesy of Steelman Photographics.*

Right: Edward C. Stokes of Millville, governor from 1905 to 1908. *Courtesy of Lummis Research Library.*

An original pot furnace at Wheaton Glassworks.

Working on the engine of a World War II fighter at Millville Airport. *Courtesy of Steelman Photograpics.*

World War II P-47 fighter plane at Millville. *Courtesy of Steelman Photographics.*

and educational interests of the people. Organized by the workingmen on the basis of improving their leisure hours, it was founded largely on the basis of entertainment." Hard liquor was not available at the institute.

The new building and furniture cost $23,000, and R. Pearsall Smith, a member of the board of Whitall Tatum, put up $5,000 in advance and pledged an additional sum "at a low rate of interest." According to Cushing and Sheppard, "The institute itself raised, by subscription, members' dues and entertainments, $2,500. Members' dues and the baths are expected to pay the expenses." The annual tax was just $1.

Located on the first floor of the building was a clubroom fitted with chairs and tables where checkers, chess and other games were played to "amuse the crowd nightly. Music and singing are heard." The historians reported that nightly attendance in the clubroom was more than one hundred men. "The noise is social, not boisterous."

Next to the clubroom was a library that included more than two thousand volumes. Readers also could sit down with newspapers from New York and Philadelphia. While the clubroom was for men only, the library was also used by women and children, presumably family members related to the workingmen. Average attendance in the library was sixty.

On the second floor was a large hall that could accommodate five hundred people. The hall was equipped with a stage, scenery and two dressing rooms.

The hall was used mostly for amateur play performances, exhibits of the schoolchildren's work and meetings of the local Woman's Christian Temperance Union. Cushing and Sheppard pointed out that the WCTU meetings were attended by people "who rarely attend a temperance meeting in a church." They also mentioned that the WCTU paid a rental fee that "affords a large income" for the institute. Presumably, that income may have allowed Whithall Tatum to cut back on its financing commitment.

Whithall Tatum was particularly proud of its commitment to industrial education of young men in Millville. On the upper floor of the building were four classrooms that were used every evening by classes for men needing basic instruction.

Fourteen years before the founding of the Workingman's Institute, in 1868, a sizable group of Millville men formed the Manumuskin Tribe of the International Order of Red Men. The IORM, which originated in the East and then established tribes across the country, traced its history to the Boston Tea Party, when young men dressed as Indians called themselves Sons of Liberty and threw a ship's cargo of British tea into the harbor. Indeed, members of the Millville chapter often dressed as Indians for meetings and other functions.

East Lake Mill, circa 1910. *Courtesy of Lummis Research Library.*

The first officers of the Millville chapter were John W. Newlin, James M. Wells, Samuel H. Ortlip and Henry Bornhoff. In the late nineteenth century, the lodge reported that it "has had a prosperous career and now numbers 120 members." The lodge also boasted that it had a surplus in its treasury of "almost" $600.

Although Millville no longer has an IORM tribe, tribes still exist in New Jersey at Egg Harbor, Little Egg Harbor, Northvale and Tuckerton.

Chapter 24

LONG AGO IN STOW CREEK TOWNSHIP

Once upon a bad time in Cumberland County and much of the rest of southern New Jersey, farmers plowed the same fields and planted the same crops year after year after year until they wore out the land, pretty much depleting it of any nutrients. Then, in the first decades of the nineteenth century, they discovered that their land could be enriched and their crops saved by a mudlike substance in the ground that they called marl. A lot of that crop-enriching, farm-saving marl was discovered in pits along Stow Creek and its branches. Most of Stow Creek Township's residents continue to live and manage productive farms.

Long before farmers discovered marl along the banks of Stow Creek, other men found ways to put Stow Creek itself to good use. One of the first to do so was John Brick, a native of England, who purchased one thousand acres bordering the creek in 1680. Of course, he knew nothing about the marl, but it didn't matter because his interest was in generating power for sawmills and gristmills that he had constructed by the turn of the century. The area where the mills were located became known as Jericho. Today, Jericho is simply a crossroads in Stow Creek Township, but in the eighteenth and nineteenth centuries, it was where the mills flourished.

As a mill town, Jericho was an important place in the early history of both Cumberland and Salem Counties. Another enterprising businessman, John S. Wood, took over the mills in the early 1800s, and Jericho—and Stow Creek Township—continued to prosper. Referred to as "an enterprising, active businessman," Wood "endeavored to build up the place," according to

The old Jericho Hotel as it appeared circa 1890. *Courtesy of Lummis Research Library.*

Thomas Cushing and Charles Sheppard. "Among other projects, he converted the distillery belonging to him into a woolen factory in the spring of 1818, associating himself in the business with John E. Jeffers, who had been in that business for a number of years in New York State. Machinery was put in for the manufacture of broadcloths, cassimeres, satinets, etc." Unfortunately, Mr. Jeffers was either a bad businessman or was uncomfortable living in Stow Creek (or both). In any event, he left town, and the business he had set up closed down.

Other mills were built in the township, one being the Seventh-day Mill, which got its name from the Seventh-day Adventists who populated Stow Creek and Hopewell Townships. Smalley's Saw-Mill, which was built on Bishop's Run, a branch of Stow Creek, was owned by Isaac M. Smalley, and in the latter quarter of the nineteenth century, it was turning out custom work and prospering.

The men who conceived, built and prospered from the mills in that area of Stow Creek known as Jericho were later bested in terms of fame and fortune by Maskell Ware, who designed chairs, and Charles Hires, who made root beer.

Maskell Ware, who was ten years old when America declared its independence, was the first in a very long line of Wares and an equally long line of expert makers of handcrafted, slat-backed and rush-bottomed chairs. According to Deborah D. Waters, author of *Wares and Chairs*, "[The chairs] associated with Maskell Ware of Roadstown and his descendants have excited collectors of American furniture aesthetically for more than fifty years. As examples of the persistence and longevity of traditional craft forms such chairs have also interested furniture historians."

Unfortunately, wrote Ms. Waters, neither Maskell nor his successors in the Ware family left many records that trace the family's history as expert craftsmen. What Ware family history there is, when charted, outlines *the accommodations made by one group of traditional craftsmen to modernizing society.*

Maskell Ware was the first of 23 Ware family members active in some phase of the chair and furniture trades. He was the third son of Marcy Moore and Elanthan Ware and was apprenticed to John Lanning, a Greenwich chairmaker and farmer. Maskell Ware married Hannah Simpkins in 1789 and settled in Roadstown, a village of 20 dwellings "peopled principally by the cultivators of the soil."

In those early years, Ware couldn't make and sell enough chairs to support his family of eleven children, so he spent more time working as a farmer than as a craftsman. Of course, as history records, the Ware successors and craftsmen continued to make and sell the chairs that still excite collectors.

Perhaps the only agreed-on facts concerning Charles Hires are that he grew up on his family's farm in Stow Creek Township; that his root beer (first called root tea) originally combined twenty-five roots, herbs and berries; and that he made a fortune selling Hires Root Beer. One reliable source even alleged that Hires Root Beer was *not* the first such product on the market. According to Dr. E. Sortomme, "There are some cook books in the Library of Congress that have recipes for root beer from 10 to 20 years before [Hires] began to sell his version [in 1876 at the World's Fair in Philadelphia]."

Of course, Dr. Sortomme's version differs markedly from others, particularly those advanced by local historians. For example, Joseph DeLuca of the Bridgeton Antiquarian League claims Hires experimented with various brews while still living on the family farm in Roadstown. On the other hand, some Millville historians alleged that Hires, while still a teenager, experimented with various concoctions while working in a confectionery store in Millville. One story (fable?) suggested that Hires was "inspired" to invent root beer by an "eccentric" relative who wandered the woods collecting various barks and roots.

Charles Hires's obituary gave even another account about how a simple farm boy from Stow Creek, New Jersey, came to invent root beer. According to the obituary, Reverend Dr. Russell Conwell, founder of Temple University, asked Hires to help him concoct a tasty beverage that might convince hard drinkers to give up alcoholic beverages.

Again, the facts that everyone agrees with are that Charles Hires was born and raised as a child in Stow Creek Township and generally has been credited with conceiving and profiting from Hires Root Beer. Oops! According to *The Press* of Atlantic City, a descendant of Charles's by the name of William L. Hires said that his ancestor was born in Elsinboro. Ah well.

Chapter 25

LONG AGO IN UPPER DEERFIELD TOWNSHIP

According to F. Alan Campbell, author of the book *A Place Called Home* about Upper Deerfield, the township was created out of Deerfield Township in 1922:

> *For nearly 200 years there was only one actual village in all of old Deerfield Township which supplied the essentials for an independent existence for the residents of the area. That was Deerfield Street. Because it is somewhat unusual for the name of a town, questions concerning its origin have been frequently asked. The answer is simple.*
>
> *After a Presbyterian meetinghouse and school were erected in 1737, several homes were built near them and eventually a general store and tavern completed the requirements for village life. Perhaps anxious to achieve equal status with Greenwich and Bridgetown, the road through this settlement became known as the "Street," the only street in Deerfield Township. Local residents would indicate their proposed destination by stating that they were headed for the "Street," just as the people of today announce they are going "downtown," meaning Bridgeton, or to the "city," referring to Philadelphia.*

Campbell reminded his readers that Deerfield Street continues to be an acceptable designation for Upper Deerfield Township, or at least the northern section of it.

Long before the townships split, in the middle of the eighteenth century, Recompense Leake built his house in what is now Upper

Van Meeks family—Ephraim, Emma and Anna—on Centerton Road in Upper Deerfield. *Courtesy of Lummis Research Library.*

Deerfield. According to Campbell, a visitor to the house could pretty much determine the date of construction by going up into the attic and observing the beams "employing mortise and pin construction as well as the hand hewn adze marks on the beams and vestiges of bark remaining on the members." Leake was a member of the township committee and the county board of freeholders. His son, Nathan, married Hannah Fithian, who was a first cousin to Philip Vickers Fithian, a prominent Patriot in the 1770s who played a major role in the tea burning at Greenwich.

Most of the early settlers of what became Upper Deerfield, families like the Leakes, originated in the British Isles and Ireland. Other early pioneers came from Sweden. However, beginning with the late 1910s and early 1920s of the twentieth century, Upper Deerfield became home to men, women and children from many countries and cultures who spoke many languages. For example, when Upper Deerfield separated from Deerfield Township in 1922, a number of the families working on the farms in the area had originated in Italy. The great majority of them were employed by C.F. Seabrook at his Seabrook Farms.

"From the mid-Nineteenth Century until 1930, Italy was a country of mass emigration," I wrote in my book *Growing a Global Village*, "most of it to the United States. In 1913 alone, the year C.F. [Seabrook] created Seabrook Farms, 565,000 Italians emigrated to this country." A good number of these Italians were single men who may have been escaping service in the army during World War I. "As the war was winding down, a number of the single Italian men working at Seabrook Farms set sail for Italy, only to return shortly thereafter with a wife and sometimes a child or two. Other workers married daughters of Italian families who had settled in south Philadelphia. Then, in the early 1920s, still more Italian immigrant men and their families arrived at Seabrook Farms." As a result, Seabrook built what became known as the Italian Village.

The hiring and housing of Italian workers and their families was just a beginning for Seabrook Farms and Upper Deerfield. Just before the advent of World War II and for some years during and after the war, Seabrook Farms employed and housed men and women from many regions and countries. Again from *Growing a Global Village*:

> *Among those men and women joining the ever-larger workforce and taking up residence in the global village* [created by Seabrook Farms in the township for the expanding workforce] *were transplants from the foothills of the Great Smoky Mountains in Tennessee. From 1943 to 1946, recruiting efforts extended into the Deep South and zeroed in on female African-American college students. Toward the end of May in each of those years Seabrook hired thirty or more women and flew them north out of Atlanta, accompanied by chaperones supplied by the company.*

Seabrook Farms was at its busiest during and immediately after World War II. Those were days when modern equipment had not yet replaced manual labor. Therefore, the company looked far and wide for employees to work in the many fields and various buildings. One of the largest contingents of new employees was two thousand or so Japanese Americans recruited from the interment camps out west, where they had been contained behind barbed wire by the United States government shortly after the bombing of Pearl Harbor.

Although the Japanese Americans were the first Asians to be included in the workforce [and the population of Upper Deerfield], they joined a global village in the making. Already in the mix [by 1942] were Italians, Jamaicans and others from the West Indies, workers from Tennessee, coal miners from West Virginia, local African Americans, and a few Russians, Poles and Dutch People. After the war, Seabrook Farms recruited

Estonians, Latvians and Lithuanians direct from refugee camps in Europe, and the global village(s)—in which the men, women and children from other states and countries now far outnumbered the longtime residents of Upper Deerfield—continued to grow.

As one might expect, the many cultures and races represented in the workforce of Seabrook Farms were also represented in the public school serving the children of those workers:

> *In 1947, New Jersey passed a law prohibiting racial segregation in its public schools, thus becoming the first state in the nation to do so. Of course, the Charles F. Seabrook School had been desegregated since its opening twenty-two years earlier, and in the late 1940s its classrooms contained not only children of African American and West Indies employees of Seabrook Farms, but also Japanese American and Estonian children. By the mid-1950s, the school would enroll boys and girls whose roots tapped twenty-five nationalities or cultures. The Seabrook School in the first half of the Twentieth Century was unlike almost any other school in rural America.*

In March 1972, the C.F. Seabrook Company put before the Upper Deerfield Township Committee a plan for developing what was to be called an agri-city, consisting of six thousand acres with an estimated population of forty-five thousand people. According to Alan Palmer:

> *That project did not come to fruition for a number of reasons. The company was not able to attract industrial developers to the area, nor was existing transportation adequate to make an agri-city accessible to the larger urban centers. Even though "Farmingtown" (as the agri-city would have been known) never was built, throughout the 1950s and until the present [1985], many hundreds of acres of forest or marginal land have been developed into housing sites. Collectively, these small developments may be thought of as an "Agri-City," not as dreamed by its promoters, but providing the advantages of country life while remaining free from the congestion and other disadvantages of a city environment.*

Chapter 26

LONG AGO IN VINELAND

Perhaps the better title for this chapter would be "Long Ago in the Mind, Heart and Hands of Charles Kline Landis." It was Landis, after all, who conceived the city of Vineland, planned it and pretty much controlled it (or tried to) during the latter decades of the nineteenth century.

Landis was the son of a prosperous Philadelphia family and trained as a lawyer. Beginning when he was just twenty-four years old, he demonstrated what could be accomplished by a person with big ideas and a big bank account. In 1857, he and a partner purchased five thousand acres lying between Philadelphia and Atlantic City along the Camden & Atlantic Railroad that became Hammonton.

Building on the success of this venture, Landis purchased more than twenty thousand acres farther south four years later with the intention of building a kind of utopia, what eventually would become the seed of Vineland. The historians Thomas Cushing and Charles Sheppard quoted Landis in later years recalling how he conceived his plan for what initially became Landis Township:

> *I decided that all the roads should be broad and straight and at right angles, making up for the want of the picturesque in the straight line and right angle by requiring trees for shade, in single or double rows, to be planted along the roads. It was required that the purchaser* [of building lots] *should erect a habitation not nearer than twenty feet from the side of the street in the city plat, or seventy-five feet from the roadside in the country.*

Downtown Vineland. *Courtesy of Steelman Photographics.*

> *The stipulation about setting houses back removed them from dust and induced great attention to the ornamenting of front gardens with flowers and shrubbery. The next stipulation was that the roadsides should be seeded to grass within two years and kept seeded. Another important question was with regard to the sale of liquor. I believed that if the public sale of liquor was stopped, both in taverns and beer-saloons, the knife would reach the root of the evil* [drunkenness]. *The local-option law in Vineland has been practically in operation since the beginning of the settlement, although the act of the* [state] *Legislature empowering the people of Landis Township to vote upon license or no license was not passed until 1864.*

This was the act that created Vineland as a township, according to Cushing and Sheppard.

In 1861, before Landis Township was official and when those newly purchased twenty thousand acres or so were still woods, Landis advertised his "new settlement" as far and wide as media and person-to-person testimony allowed at that time. By the end of that year, only half a dozen settlers had responded to Landis's promotion. The first responder was J.G. Colson, who in October of that year bought ten acres along what became West Railroad Boulevard above Oak Road. After Colson came George L. Post, who bought forty acres on the southeast corner of the future Main and Post Roads.

Landis sold more land and welcomed more new residents in the following year, 1862. During that year, Landis Avenue (which, when finally completed, would measure one hundred feet across) was cleared of tree stumps. Cushing and Sheppard reported more progress: "Main Avenue, leading to Millville, was straightened and widened, and other streets were opened. The first hotel was opened by C.P. Davis. A schoolhouse was erected, and a private school opened by Miss Lucille Richardson, with eleven scholars."

Every train brought new arrivals, and improvements began in all directions. Lands were cleared and put under cultivation, and the demand for dwelling houses was greater than could be supplied. In the one month of January 1865, more than one thousand acres of wild land were sold, and as the plans of Mr. Landis divided the land into small farms averaging not more than fifteen or twenty acres each, this represents quite an addition to the population in the one month.

Continued Cushing and Sheppard: "Many of the newcomers were among the best citizens of the land, and quite a number were wealthy. These were attracted to Vineland by its fame as a temperance town and the mildness of the climate as compared with that of New England and the Northwest. In 1866, more than 1,200 buildings were erected."

The place where people were settling became known as Vineland mainly because of the vineyards encouraged by Landis and established early on primarily by Italian growers. Landis offered growers twenty acres of land that they had to clear and use for the growing of grapes. Of course, they were not allowed to make wine from those grapes. Remember, Landis insisted on his town being a dry town.

Landis carefully planned the city of Vineland:

In addition to banning the sale of alcohol, Landis required that purchasers of land in Vineland had to build a house on the purchased property within a year of purchase, that 2½ acres of the often heavily-wooded land had to be cleared and farmed each year, and that adequate space be placed between houses and roads to allow for planting of flowers and shade trees along the routes through town. The added space between houses helped ensure that if a family were to contract a disease, it would have significantly less chance of becoming an outbreak than if they were closer together.

While Landis encouraged grape growers in particular, the land was also well suited to other growers and farmers. According to Cushing and Sheppard, "The soil of Vineland seeming well adapted to the growth of grapes, pears and other small fruits, large vineyards, orchards and berry patches were set out shortly after the first arrivals [of settlers], and these constitute [in the 1800s] the leading crops of Vineland." By the 1880s, farmers growing and selling fruits were prospering. In 1881, for example, 250,000 quarts of strawberries were shipped. They brought $25,000. During the same period, blackberries sold netted $70,000. One of the primary purchasers of grapes grown by Vineland farmers was Thomas Bramwell Welch.

As Vineland expanded and developed in the latter decades of the nineteenth century, it attracted a variety of people with an even greater variety of beliefs and causes. For example, in July 1864, a group of citizens formed an organization or sect called Friends of Progress. It included Friends (Quakers), spiritualists, agnostics and the occasional atheist. The organization built Plum Street Hall, where members could discuss and debate a wide variety of ideas and positions. Among those organizations that sponsored controversial programs and speakers at Plum Street Hall were the Equal Rights and Universal Peace Association and the Committee of Resolutions for the State Suffrage Convention. Speakers at Plum Street Hall included Susan B. Anthony, the primary spokesperson for women's suffrage, and Frederick Douglass, who championed the causes of African Americans.

Unfortunately, the latter 1800s also included what many called the "crime of the century." The historians Cushing and Sheppard described what happened:

> *An opposition to the management of township affairs, as they were carried on by Mr. Landis and his friends, gradually grew up and was voiced by the* Independent, *edited by Uri Carruth. Mr. Carruth carried the opposition to extremes, and indulged in a series of personal attacks on Mr. Landis, criticisms of his policy and ridicule of his public and private acts. On March 19, 1875, Mr. Landis, after reading the issue of the* Independent *containing an article which ridiculed Mrs. Landis as well as himself, went to the office of Mr. Carruth. There were no witnesses to the meeting in the office. In a few moments, Mr. Carruth rushed into the printing department, followed by Mr. Landis, who fired at him, the bullet entering the back of Mr. Carruth's head. Mr. Landis gave himself up and was committed to jail to await the results of the injury.*

Landis Avenue in Vineland, circa late 1800s or early 1900s. *Courtesy of Lummis Research Library.*

Mr. Carruth recovering, Mr. Landis was admitted to bail. It was thought Mr. Carruth would entirely recover, but he died before the expiration of a year from abscesses which formed around the bullet. Mr. Landis was recommitted to jail and was tried at the adjourned January term, 1876, of the Court of Oyer and Terminer of Cumberland County, Judge Alfred Reed presiding. After a long and tedious trial, the jury returned a verdict of not guilty on the plea of temporary insanity. It was the most noted criminal trial in the history of the county.

Before Vineland became a city, it was a borough. Before that, it was a township, and before that, it was Landis's twenty thousand acres, but it wasn't easy becoming a borough. In May 1880, an election was held to decide whether Vineland would become a borough under state law. The vote was 181 in favor and 122 against. An explanation of why 122 persons voted against the township becoming a borough could not be found. In any event, in that same year, the population of Mr. Landis's Vineland was 2,519.

BIBLIOGRAPHY

American Glass Review. "He Started Glass Making in Millville." April 14, 1934.

Barber, John W., and Henry Howe. *Cumberland County from Historical Collections of the State of New Jersey.* N.p.: S. Tuttle, 1844.

Barsotti, Debra A. "Maurice River Recollection Project: Janice and Jeanette Burcham; Twin Efforts to Preserve an Icon." Citizens United to Protect the Maurice River and Its Tributaries, 2002.

Bridgeton Evening News. "The Oystermen of Cumberland County." September 8, 1910.

Cushing, Thomas, and Charles E. Sheppard. *History of the Counties of Gloucester, Salem and Cumberland New Jersey.* N.p.: Everts & Peck, 1893.

Dahlgren, Stellan, and Hans Norman. *The Rise and Fall of New Sweden.* N.p.: Almqvist & Wiksell International, 1988.

Elmer, Lucius Q.C. *History of the Early Settlement and Progress of Cumberland County.* N.p.: George F. Nixon, 1869.

Gerlach, Larry R., ed. *New Jersey in the American Revolution, 1763–1783: A Documentary History.* Trenton: New Jersey Historical Commission, 1975.

Harrison, Charles H. *Growing a Global Village: Making History at Seabrook Farms.* New York: Holmes & Meier, 2003.

History of the Eastern Oyster. N.p.: New Jersey Division of Fish & Wildlife, 2001.

Jewish Encyclopedia. New York: Funk & Wagnalls, 1901.

Jones, Jean. "Old-Timers Recall Oyster Boats." *News of Cumberland County,* October 23, 1999.

Lee, Francis B. *New Jersey as a Colony and as a State: One of the Original Thirteen.* N.p.: Publishing Society of New Jersey, 1903.

McCormick, Richard P. *New Jersey from Colony to State, 1609–1789.* Princeton, NJ: D. Van Nostrand Company, 1964.

National Park Service. "Economics of Land Reclamation." Chap. 4 in *Historic Themes and Resources within the New Jersey Coastal Heritage Trail Route.* N.p.: n.d.

————. "Industry, Southern New Jersey and the Delaware Bay." Chap. 5 in *Historic Themes and Resources within the New Jersey Coastal Heritage Trail Route.* N.p.: n.d.

————. "Maritime Activities." Chap. 3 in *Historic Themes and Resources within the New Jersey Coastal Heritage Trail Route.* N.p.: n.d.

Nichols, Isaac T. *Historic Days in Cumberland County.* Bridgeton, NJ, 1907.

Palmer, F. Alan. *The Place Called Home: An Illustrated History of the Township of Upper Deerfield.* Seabrook, NJ: Upper Deerfield Township Committee, 1985.

Pepper, Adeline. *Glass Gaffers of New Jersey and Their Creations from 1739 to the Present.* New York: Scribner Books, 1971.

Robbins, Paula Ivaska. *The Travels of Peter Kalm.* Fleischmanns, NY: Purple Mountain Press, 2007.

Sebold, Kimberly R. *From Marsh to Farm: The Landscape Transformation of Coastal New Jersey.* Washington, D.C.: National Park Service, Department of Interior, 2005.

Stewart, Frank H. *Salem County in the Revolution.* Salem, NJ: Salem County Historical Society, 1967.

Vanaman, Herbert W. "Glass Making at Port Elizabeth." *Vineland Historical Magazine* (July–October 1965).

Wikipedia. "Whitall Tatum Company." http://en.wikipedia.org/wiki/Whitall_Tatum_Company.

ABOUT THE AUTHOR

In addition to writing this history of Cumberland County, Charles H. Harrison has written the books *Salem County: A Story of People* (The History Press), *Growing a Global Village: The Story of Seabrook Farms* (Holmes & Meier) and *Tending the Garden State* (Rutgers University Press). He also has written a number of articles about New Jersey and its people for such magazines as *Trailer Life*, *Planning*, *New Jersey Monthly* and *South Jersey*. Harrison and his wife reside in a 150-year-old house in Woodstown. Original photographs for this book were taken by Stephan A. Harrison of Pitman. Stephan was a photographer for *Today's Sunbeam* in Salem County.

Visit us at
www.historypress.net